Strategic Communication and Deformative Transparency

T0299968

This book illustrates commonly used discourses of extremists, radicals, and organizations advocating for difficult causes. Emergent communication technologies enhance the outrageous character of images and metaphorical expressions aimed to capture the imagination, attention, and interest of distracted and increasingly fragmented audiences. Dr. Nahon-Serfaty's strong academic and professional authority adds legitimacy to this innovative scholarship.

—Juan-Carlos Molleda, University of Oregon, USA

This book examines deformative transparency and its different manifestations in political communication, propaganda and public health. The objective is to present the theoretical foundations of deformative transparency, as grotesque and *esperpentic* transparency, and illustrate the validity of such approach to understand the strategic and ethical implications of the proactive disclosure of the "shocking", "ugly" or "outside the norm". Four areas are discussed: political communication with particular focus on such populist politicians as the deceased Venezuelan president Hugo Chávez; the campaign and presidency of Donald Trump; the tenure in office of the mayor of Toronto, Rob Ford; propaganda strategies of Islamist terrorist organizations such as the Islamic State's escalation of the visually horrific; and public health campaigns that use "disturbing images" to promote public awareness and eventually influence behavioural change. This study on the transparently grotesque is part of a research program about the economy of emotions in public communication.

Isaac Nahon-Serfaty is Associate Professor in the Department of Communication at the University of Ottawa, Canada.

Routledge Focus on Communication Studies

A Relational Model of Public Discourse
The African Philosophy of Ubuntu
Leyla Tavernaro-Haidarian

Communicating Science and Technology through Online Video
Researching a New Media Phenomenon
Edited by Bienvenido León and Michael Bourk

Strategic Communication and Deformative Transparency
Persuasion in Politics, Propaganda, and Public Health
Isaac Nahon-Serfaty

Strategic Communication and Deformative Transparency

Persuasion in Politics, Propaganda, and Public Health

Isaac Nahon-Serfaty

Routledge
Taylor & Francis Group

LONDON AND NEW YORK

First published 2019
by Routledge

2 Park Square, Milton Park, Abingdon, Oxfordshire OX14 4RN
52 Vanderbilt Avenue, New York, NY 10017

Routledge is an imprint of the Taylor & Francis Group, an informa business

First issued in paperback 2020

Library of Congress Cataloging-in-Publication Data
A catalog record for this book has been requested

ISBN: 978-1-138-65665-9 (hbk)
ISBN: 978-0-367-60679-4 (pbk)

Typeset in Times New Roman
by Apex CoVantage, LLC

Ô flots abracadabrantesques . . .
Arthur Rimbaud

Lift up your eyes
Look around you,
Here it is!
I see,
the eyes of any child see
how the guts and intestines
of the strong sensations
hang from the belly of the cinematography
that the spur of the revolution has pierced . . .

Dziga Vertov

Contents

Figures

Acknowledgements

I would like to thank the people who contributed to the drafting of this volume, either by participating in the development and evolution of the text, or by signalling some of the theoretical lacunas, that I hope I was able to fill. To my Venezuelan colleagues Colette Capriles, Néstor Garrido, Erick Del Bufalo, Paula Vásquez, and Manuel Silva-Ferrer who enriched my vision about the aesthetics of the *chavista* politics. To Miguel Angel Karam, Luisa Torrealba, and Juan Carlos Molleda who invited me to discuss these ideas with their students in Toluca, Caracas, and Gainesville. To Rasmus Kleis Nielsen who introduced me to the notion of social performance. To Catalina Arango who helped me with the research of the case studies that illustrate the theory of grotesque transparency. And finally, to Laura Cummings who edited and improved the text in English.

Visual Preface

Figure 0.1 Cyril Winter, Anti-Abortion Activist

Photo: Isaac Nahon-Serfaty

This is a photograph (Figure a) of Cyril Winter, an Ottawa-based anti-abortion activist. I took this photo on September 8, 2017. He was in front of the Canadian Tribute to Human Rights monument, during one of his usual one-man protests.

This photo summarizes the aim and scope of this book. The bottom panel's image of body parts—of foetuses or babies, depending where you position yourself in the debate—is a clear display of grotesque transparency. Its intent is stated in its text: "No censorship". Its crudeness does not leave any room for euphemisms. Mr. Winter is not talking about "reproductive rights", "medical procedures", "the right to choose", "interrupted pregnancy", or even "pro-life". He wants to shock the public by disclosing the concrete "truth", or at least his truth.

At the heart of his message is an aesthetics of horror. It seems, however, that the image of small, dismembered bodies was not enough for Mr. Winter. To emphasize this disclosure of a crude reality, he also added the baby doll hanging from his neck. This is a sign of over-production of meaning, where the grotesque and the kitschy tend to overlap. It also reveals an economy of the affects, done through the saturation of emotions based on the premise that overcoming "cognitive indifference" requires an aesthetic reflexivity, or an alternative path to "knowing" about an issue.

The photo also speaks to the tension between strategy and tactics. Mr. Winter was present at the monument as an individual without any institutional affiliation. His means appeared to be quite limited, with no major strategic relevance. As with many cases in today's digital sphere, however, he was introducing the transparently grotesque in the public space to disrupt and eventually call attention to it. His rationale was not that different from the old prescriptions of propaganda, though he was also facing a highly overcrowded and fragmented communication ecosystem, as illustrated by passers-by at the monument who were plugged into their mobile devices.

By putting on this display, Mr. Winter visually desecrated the sacred in order to defend what he thought is the "supreme good": human life. We can assume he considered this a legitimate means to achieve his goal (that is, to end or limit abortion). Some may agree with him; others may find these images repulsive or an unethical manipulation of emotions. The majority of passers-by that day near the human rights monument were indifferent to Mr. Winter's images and speech. The question remains: how far can someone go to achieve their goals? What are the limits of the visible? This book is an attempt to answer these questions by looking into both the visible and invisible aspects of the strategy of the transparently grotesque.

Introduction

This book is about the limits of the visible. In an era of visual excesses, the physical, psychological, and social barriers that prevent us from seeing certain realities are constantly pierced by all kinds of images. Everything could potentially be seeing. This includes the sublime and the beautiful, but also the horrible, the dreadful, and the disgusting. Our access to these diverse, aesthetic ocular experiences is not new; however, the exuberance of the offer is. An overproduction of the visible has flooded the communication ecosystem, making it almost impossible *not* to see. The temptation of seeing is also nourished by the multiplication of these images. This almost physical or perceptual pressure pushes the borders of the visible and forces its limits to disintegrate. This could be compared to the situation described by Elias Canetti (1978) in *Crowds and Power*, where he talks about the fear of being touched and the conditions that allow this fear to be suppressed:

> It is only in a crowd that man can become free of this fear of being touched. This is the only situation in which the fear changes into its opposite. The crowd he needs is the dense crowd, in which is pressed to body; a crowd, too, whose physical constitution is also dense, or compact, so that he no longer notices who it is that presses against him. As soon as a man has surrendered himself to the crowd, he ceases to fear its touch.
>
> (p. 15)

A space filled with images presents the problem of choice. What should we see? According to Canetti's argument, this choice is made following the multitude's "compact and comforting" influence. It is necessary here to clarify what we mean by the multitude and how this notion relates to Canetti's views on the crowd. In this case, we can follow the definition advanced by Hardt and Negri (2004), which considers the multitude as a social entity that "remains multiple and internally different" but that is "able to act in common" (p. 100). Canetti's conception of the crowd is somewhat different; for him, those who become part of it "get rid of their differences and feel equal" (Canetti, 1978, p. 17). These two conceptualizations coincide in that social bodies have the ability to coordinate their actions, and can eventually move together towards a common direction to achieve a goal (Canetti, Ibid., p. 29). The multitude tends to behave in coordination under the impulse of their passions or affects, or in Spinoza's (1677/2014) terms:

> so that as persuade themselves, that the multitude or the men distracted by politics can even be induced to live according to the bare dictate by reason, must be dreaming of the poetic golden age, or a stage play.
>
> (Introduction, paragraph 5)

It is through the multitude's chameleonic mechanism of adaptation and imitation that certain images will be seen because they are cherished by some or hated by others. This is evident today in the production and reproduction of images in digital networks. The multitude makes the images visible and acceptable thanks to the reproductive dynamics of these networks. From a strategic point of view, the limits of the visible are defined by a quantity of spectators. The choice to show something is determined by the goal for reaching the multitude. It is not a matter of size, especially in an era of media and audience fragmentation where the public is more often approached as niches than a homogeneous totality. Instead, the goal is to reach the critical number of those who will are willing to see the image. The multitude, then, is conceived as a cluster that will become qualitatively and quantitatively "compact and comforting" enough to push the limits of the visible.

The acceptability of the visually grotesque—the subject of this book—is related to the multitude's legitimizing power. This explains why the grotesque is overly present in today's public sphere, though with variable ethical appreciations. Videos showing hostage beheadings by radical militants, pictures of the former mayor of Toronto smoking crack, photographs of a fashion model's emaciated body used as part of a campaign to denounce anorexia, and images of a dying lung-cancer patient on a cigarette package all represent different aspects of this exuberance of the horrible, the disgusting, or the out-of-the-norm. All of them are justified as truthful representations of "reality". These images are also rationalized as the best or most effective way to disclose that reality to the public. The alibi of the multitude—the multitude that should be exposed to the disrupting truth—is used to explain when and why it is morally acceptable to push some limits and become transparently grotesque. The multitude is also the receptacle that relays these images, making them acceptable through the dynamics of reproduction and imitation in an era of digital networks.

Are these shocking images truly transparent as truthful representations? That is the claim made by those producing and diffusing them. Their rhetoric, with its varied political and policy nuances, justifies breaking the limits of the visible as a way to proactively disclose the truth. The value of what they show resides in their combination of cognitive and aesthetic features. Knowing the truth, rationalize the organizations behind this kind of strategy, requires mediation of the affective driver. By emphasizing the ocular disruption (i.e., seeing things as "they are"), however, the grotesque transparency strategy prompts several theoretical and practical questions. The main objective of this book is to answer these questions.

What is a manifestation of grotesque transparency? In what way is public communication sometimes both grotesque and transparent? Chapter 1 sets out the conceptual contours of this duality, which we will also call "deformative transparency".[1] I begin by discussing the tensions between transparency and opacity, in particular criticizing the very idea of a radical opposition between total disclosure and total occultation. I understand transparency as a constructed impression, a performed and partial disclosure of a situation or information. In all self-declared transparency strategies, there is an element of opacity. This becomes evident when the disclosure performance is focused on the visually deformed or disturbing that represents, according to the genealogy of the grotesque established by Kayser (1966), a challenge to the norm or the "order of things". Being disturbed by the grotesque presupposes a lack of clarity, given that the grotesque itself implies a certain obscurity.

But what can be considered grotesque? Two theoretical keys will help us define it: first, Bakhtin's (1984) conceptualization of the "out of norm" from his study on *Rabelais and His World*; second, the notion of *esperpento* (or *esperpentic*) introduced by Spanish author Valle-Inclán (1981) as a theatrical genre centred on the deformed reflection of the hero's image in the concave mirrors. For the purpose of this study, the grotesque refers to the shift from the ideal to the material as seen in the degradation of a body or earth. More precisely, the grotesque is considered *esperpentic* in the context of public communication because of the mediation process's deformative effect and the anti-heroic character of its narrative. In this regard, the metaphor of an aquarium is also discussed as a heuristic image of the transparently grotesque's duality, a manufactured reality where fishes, plants, and rocks look truthful through the deformative mediation of the water and glass.

In Chapter 1, I also review two additional conceptual considerations about grotesque transparency. The realistically grotesque is also an expression of an aesthetic reflexivity; it is foremost an affective trigger but also functions as an alternative path to participate in the public sphere, and is not only the result of the multitude's manipulation of the affects. Furthermore, I consider this reflexivity both an input and an outcome of the social construction of value. This takes place through inter-subjective interactions in an economy of affects that, in the case of the grotesque, makes the ugly or the disgusting worthy at both the reproductive and axiological levels.

Chapter 2 moves to the more concrete aspects of the politics of affects. This is the first test in terms of how well grotesque transparency can function as an analytical framework to reveal the nuts and bolts of a disturbing disclosure strategy. Three cases from different socio-political and cultural contexts are used to illustrate the relevance of this analysis: the authoritarian populism of deceased Venezuelan president Hugo Chávez; the shocking revelation about then-presidential candidate Donald Trump's dismissive remarks regarding women; and the public disclosure of former Toronto mayor Rob Ford smoking crack. Besides their obvious particularities, these manifestations are grounded in the same strategy that points to forms of public deliberation as social drama (Alexander, 2014). In these cases, the contribution of the grotesque transparency framing resides in its emphasis on the aesthetics of an unsettling truth. The body—as a representation of the materially concrete that displaces ideal aspects of a dogma or doctrine—is at the heart of the politicization of the horrible or disgusting.

In Chapter 3, I consider the tensions between the sacred and the profane in grotesque transparency, by looking at propaganda from Islamic State (ISIS) militants and other radical organizations. The "obscurity of the religious", in the words of René Girard (1972/2010), sometimes manifests openly in the deformative disclosure strategy, as in Chávez's display of Bolívar's skeleton or ISIS's beheading videos. On other occasions, the religious emerges in more subtle ways to confront the public with the apocalyptic extremes of death or planetary destruction. Grotesque transparency also breaks the illusion of secularism, given that some forms of public communication (such as public health or political communication)—pretend to exclude the religious from the public sphere. By disrupting the modern illusion of secularism, ISIS and other organizations reintroduce religion, in its duality condition of sacralization and profanation, through transparent displays of terrorism.

Chapter 4 looks at the deformative transparent strategy from the point of view of public health campaigns. Institutionalized healthcare and medicine are also forms of the politics of affects in a "Foucauldian" way (Foucault, 1966), but tend to be considered legitimate and on higher moral ground than partisan or militant politics. The "common good" justifies public displays of the grotesque because they are the most cost-effective way to educate individuals about a disease or lifestyle, and eventually change their attitudes and behaviours. For example, the fight against the HIV-AIDS epidemic towards the end of the 20th century set the tone for the visually acceptable in the

Western world. Portraying a dying patient became the standard in HIV-AIDS campaigns, especially after Italian clothing brand the United Colors of Benetton used an emblematic picture of a dying man in a 1992 ad. This helped to erode a previous taboo and transformed the visually grotesque into a globally tolerable element of public campaigns. The World Health Organization (WHO) made that clear when it adopted the same strategy to fight tobacco addiction (Canadian Cancer Society, 2014). Showing rotten organs, sick individuals, and dying patients on cigarette packaging is now a common practice worldwide. This imitative turn—based on the premise that reproducing a grotesque strategy works—also extended to initiatives fighting eating disorders, including the polarized extremes of anorexia and obesity. Besides its efficacy and efficiency, the acceptability of deformative transparency in public health raises several questions about its "collateral damages". From a normative perspective, for example, how do these shocking campaigns contribute to the stigmatization of certain conditions? Or from a more practical point of view, how far should a public campaign go to overcome the public's supposed desensitization thanks to continuous exposure to the grotesque?

Chapter 5 discusses the main notions analysed in the case studies and enunciates an ethics of the invisible. It also returns to fundamental concepts such as strategy, transparency, the aesthetics of horror or the disgusting, and even the idea of public communication, to dissect them in light of the observed diverse, contradictory, and expansive manifestations of the transparently grotesque. Finally—without denying the right to show and see everything as a constitutive principle of the right to communicate—I propose to reconsider the value of an invisible that requires movement from the concrete to the abstract. Safranski's (1999) reflection about the place of human dignity as the ultimate abstraction beyond any reductionism and visual representation guides the discussion about the new taboo or the unrepresentable (Galloway, 2011; Rancière, 2007). I also reintroduce the communicative aspects behind the act of seeing together, and consider it as a social conversation that should take place when facing the problem of the transparently grotesque. Watching is a collective event, whether explicitly or implicitly, and includes mediators and mediations (Martín-Barbero, 1993). In other words, seeing the disrupting disclosure of the realistically horrific, disgusting, or unsettling requires interpretation and interpreters (Innerarity, 2011; 2010) to make sense of the visible and what may be an illusory representation of the truth.

I close the book with some reflections about the contribution of this study of grotesque transparency as a transversal and universal approach to unveil the changes and atavisms that we observe in public communication. I also propose that the analysis of this disclosure strategy can help us understand broader social, political, and cultural processes from the point of view of an aesthetic reflexivity and the economy of the affects. Finally, I envision the next stage of this research program focused on the exploration of kitsch in public communication and the strategic use of emotions.

Note

1. I prefer the term "deformative" rather than "deformed", given that it conveys the idea of a performative process and not a fixed representation of the so-called "reality".

1 Grotesque Transparency

Theoretical and Methodological Foundations

All strategy begins and ends with the body, or more precisely, with the human body. This is even more evident when we think in terms of communication strategy. Most communication scholarship emphasizes the strategy's rhetorical and discursive aspects in terms of persuasion and argumentation, particularly in public communication. I claim in this book, however, that the fundamentals of this strategic endeavor reside in the human body, using it as the focal point where affects, reasons, and actions converge. Foucault has already cited evidence to this effect, particularly in his works about prisons and hospitals as sites for domestication of the body (Foucault, 1966, 1968). But as a good inheritor of Enlightenment ideas, Foucault places too much attention on discourse and hence the power of *logos* as a disciplinary device.

Elias Canetti provides a better understanding of the body's central role in public or mass communication. In the first paragraph of his magnum opus *Crowds and Power*, Canetti (1960/1978) sets the body as the first boundary that separates the individual self from others. Why does that boundary—characterized as the fear or repulsion of being touched—fall when we accept to be part of a crowd? This is the main question Canetti (1960/1978) answers in his book. By doing so, he makes a significant contribution to the understanding of public communication. First, he reinserts the human body into the comprehension of social phenomena. Second, he approaches the collective (the crowd) not only as a collection of bodies, but as a somewhat unified body itself possessing its own logic and mechanisms. Though Canetti (1960/1978) does not state it blatantly, *Crowds and Power* challenges the classical Cartesianism that gives preeminence to the *cogito* as mind (or *esprit* in French), and thus thinking and its expression in language, over the material, affective, and "instinctive" body. In the words of Antonio Damasio (2003):

> For Descartes, the human mind remained devoid of spatial extension
> and material substance, two negative traits that made it capable of

living after the body no longer existed. It was a substance but it was not physical.

(p. 188)

In Spinozian terms, we can say that "mind and body are parallel and mutually correlated processes, mimicking each other at every crossroad, as two faces of the same thing" (Damasio, 2003, p. 217). Refocusing attention on the mind-body connection has a particular importance for the study of the grotesque in public communication. The grotesque is an expression of the body and its functions, as stated by Bakhtin (1984) in his study about Rabelais and grotesque realism. But the grotesque is also a communicative act through which the affects (i.e., expression of emotions and reaction to them) look to achieve a certain goal. In that sense, grotesque communication is always strategic as it is attached to the idea of an organization or individual manipulating the forces at play (e.g., cultural, social, economic, or political) to attain a winning position.

In an era of digital networks, how does the individual and the collective body manifest? To properly understand this question, I return to Canetti's (1960/1978) idea that the crowd, as a unit, sometimes limits itself (i.e., closed crowds) to avoid expansion; on other occasions, it is an entity that looks to grow (i.e., open crowds). The collective bodies of the digital era are also closed and open, depending on the circumstances, interests, objectives, power relations, and other factors that intervene in public communication through digital networks. "Closed crowds" limit themselves when their individuals form a "tribe", as some marketers have called them (Canetti, 1960/1978, p. 17), and activate certain loops (e.g., discursive, symbolic, imaginary, visual) to reinforce their own ideas, opinions, attitudes, and behaviours. "Open crowds" (Canetti, 1960/1978, p. 16) are expanding entities that want to attract more bodies and develop a massive, growing network.

The question remains, however, regarding the actuality of the material body in public communication via virtual spaces. Why does the body retain a place of significance in communication strategies in the virtual world, where it appears to vanish behind screens? To properly address this, we must define what we mean by virtual. Pierre Lévy (1995) has extensively studied the *virtual being*. He differentiates between the virtual and the actual as a way to explain the indissoluble link that connects virtuality and actuality. The virtual is symbolic, while the actual conveys the idea of the material. Philosophers and communication scholars recognize that for individuals, there is no way to access the actual without referring to the virtual or symbolic. In the era of "virtual communication" (as we should acknowledge that every communication is virtual, since it requires the symbolic), the body is at the heart of social, political, economic, and cultural processes. The preeminence of body-focused images in digital networks (for example, the face in selfies or *égoportrait*, as it has been cleverly translated in French) proves this. The material consequences of such communications (e.g., to consume, to vote, to adopt a healthy lifestyle, to have sex, to eat, etc.) emphasize the bodily dimension of such "virtual interactions".

The introduction of the visually grotesque in public communication research also challenges the purely spiritual, in the sense of mind-centred or rhetorical-discursive (Ihlen, 2002) traditions that tend to neglect the body's role in such processes. Paying attention to the grotesque and the "realistically grotesque" as I will discuss later in this chapter, means to analyse without prejudice the affects (or emotions as they are externalized) in the study of political, public health, or propaganda strategies. Instead of being dismissive (i.e., affects are irrational) or simply manipulative (i.e., appealing to the audience's basic instincts), I propose to build the foundation of an "economy of the affects" that will contribute to a better understanding of what is happening in political communication, health communication, propaganda, and social activism in a world where the illusion of total transparency prevails through the mediation of digital networks.

The Grotesque and the *Esperpento*

The visually grotesque disrupts the very idea of transparency, a notion that is largely praised by politicians, scholars, and militants. "Grotesque transparency" conveys a paradox since the shocking impact of the horrific, disgusting, ugly, or deformed often blurs the issue at hand and produces opacity. Is there a truly transparent grotesque? The main argument of this book is yes, the transparently grotesque is pervasively used as a strategy in different public communication manifestations because it is considered highly effective. The other argument put forward by this book is that the transparently grotesque (like transparency in general) is always mediated. That is why I consider the grotesque as *esperpento*, according to the definition of Spanish writer Ramón María del Valle-Inclán (1981). In his play *Luces de bohemia*, the dramatis personae Don Latino and Max discuss this concept (1981):

> Don Latino—The classical heroes reflected in the concave mirrors give the *Esperpento*. The tragic meaning of the Spanish life only can be achieved through an aesthetics systematically deformed [. . .] Max—Spain is a grotesque deformation of the European civilization [. . .] The most beautiful images in a concave mirror are absurd [. . .] Max—[. . .] The deformation is no longer so when is the subject of a perfect

mathematics. My current aesthetic transforms with the mathematics of the concave mirrors the classical norms.

(p. 106) (Our translation)

The *esperpento* is a theatrical genre that clearly contrasts the classical hero, who represents the norm of the beautiful and the truth, and the deformed representation accessible to the public through the deformative or mediated illumination of the concave mirrors. Valle-Inclán (1981) introduced his aesthetics of the grotesque by creating a tension between the "norm" of the "civilized word" and an "alternate" norm—the one derived from the mathematics of the concave mirrors—where another kind of reflexivity or "aesthetical reflexivity" (Lash, 1995, 1999) is possible.

What can be considered strategically grotesque? We must start by agreeing on what we mean by the "realistically grotesque". A theory of grotesque transparency will approach these public communication manifestations as expressions that are out of the norm. Here, I follow Bakhtin's (1984) definition of "grotesque realism":

> The essential principle of grotesque realism is degradation, that is, the lowering of all that is high, spiritual, ideal, abstract: it is a transfer to the material level, to the sphere of earth and body in their indissoluble unity.
>
> (p. 19)

In essence, the transparently grotesque pretends to be an accurate and truthful representation of the materially and/or idealistically degraded to which the public has access through the deformative mediation of the "concave mirrors" (Valle-Inclán, 1981, p. 106) of digital networks. It becomes strategic, as I will demonstrate in the next section, when used as the main driver to manipulate affective forces and produce a political, social, economic, or cultural outcome.

Strategy and Tactics

The grotesque as an aesthetic category has been mainly studied as a disruptive manifestation of arts and literature that is historically situated, and therefore evolves and changes according to the tastes and moral judgments of the day (Eco, 2007). Regardless of their historical context, however, representations of the grotesque always convey a certain idea or impression of the "*deformed, fantastic, ugly*" (Schevill, 1977/2009, p. 2, italics in the original) as "an attempt to invoke and subdue the demonic aspects of the world" (Kayser, 1966, p. 188).

In this book, strategy will be understood as following Certeau's (2000) definition, in clear opposition of what he considered to be the tactical. Paraphrasing Certeau (2000, pp. XLIX-L), strategy is the institutional manipulation of the forces and power rapports present in an environment (e.g., social, political, cultural, psychological), to establish a differentiated or advantageous position from where the institution manages its relationships with the public, their stakeholders, or society in a broader sense. Contrary to this, Certeau (2000) conceives of tactics as the calculation that cannot be displayed in a particular place, which takes place in another location, emphasizes space versus time, and is more focused on action than discourse.

To clarify the distinction between strategy and tactic, Certeau (2000, p. L) makes the differentiation between "owning" a stable place, from where the political, economic, or scientific rationality builds up its power according to a strategic model, and the "instability" (or the "Brownian movement") of the day-to-day or tactical practices (e.g., reading, talking, cooking, consuming, dwelling). Thus, the tactical belongs to the micro-practices through which people (e.g., users, consumers, readers, citizens) re-appropriate or reclaim the space organized by the institutional strategist (Certeau, 2000, p. XLIV). In this sense, tactics could be equated with the "anti-discipline" or the creative actions used to escape the disciplinary webs of strategy (Certeau, 2000, p. XLV).

The strategic communication of the transparently grotesque, then, is a performance that is considered both representation (strategy) and reception (tactics). In that regard, I consider the strategically grotesque a manifestation of ocular politics, where the locus has been displaced from the voice—as discursive or rhetorical expression—to the eye. Individuals often access politics or current affairs by watching others engaged in different kinds of representations or, more precisely, in social performances (Alexander, 2004). The condition of spectatorship ensures that the role played by individuals inevitably undermines the "rationality of public discourse, thus further alienating everyday citizens from the sense that they are a party of genuine political decision-making and the reasoning on which it is based" (Green, 2010, p. 5).

A more nuanced perspective may argue that the politics of spectatorship is an alternate or tactical route for participation in the public sphere. Social performance understood as drama "is fundamental to the search for meaning and solidarity in a post-ritual world [. . .]. Without drama, collective and personal meanings could not be sustained, evil could not be identified, and justice would be impossible to obtain" (Alexander, 2014, pp. 9–10). In Goffman's (1956) terms, through these representations the performer and the public accept theatrical convention and consent to being immersed in the "real reality" of engaging in an institutionalized dynamic of seduction and deception (Cooper, 1993).

The focus on the ocular emphasizes the importance of aesthetics in "spectacular politics" (Green, 2010, p. 181), given that projecting an image that fits a certain canon of beauty or even goodness is essential in such dramas. Nevertheless, it is evident that via ocular politics, individuals can also examine the ugly, grotesque, or kitschy side of politicians and politics, as these too are categories of institutional aesthetics (Strati, 1996). Aesthetics are not only pure contemplation but also sensible action, as beautifully stated by Gherardi and Strati (2017):

> aesthetic discourse on organization, means taste, sensory perception, and aesthetic judgment through the senses, imagination, and symbolic construction, mythical thinking, and poetic logic. It signifies not only art and artistic worlds but also the ordinary beauty and the ordinary ugliness that are collectively constructed even in nonartistic organizations, through negotiation of the aesthetic and the interaction among aesthetic feelings that are like the thinking of the body in a world of sensible knowing.
>
> (p. 749)

From the perspective of an aesthetic of action, grotesque transparency is a way to disclose knowledge, linking it to the experience of shock or disruption caused by an ugly but also real or authentic image.

Transparency and Opacity

To be strategically transparent is often viewed and discussed as an ideal of institutional governance (Gupta & Mason, 2014), corporate communication (Oliver, 2004), or international relations (Lord, 2006). In this sense, transparency is defined as:

> the possibility of knowing—in the name of the public's right to information—about the structures, the functioning and the actions of any given institution, either public or private.
>
> (Balle, 2006, p. 449) (Our translation)

I approach transparency as an impression currently created in large part through the *esperpentic* mediation of digital networks (Meijer, 2009, p. 256). It is also understood as an ideological construct (Libaert, 2003, p. 47) that serves institutional or corporate interests. Those engaged in transparently grotesque performances are proactively disclosing the "truth" to the public (Oliver, 2004). This theory is primarily concerned with a performed transparency that emphasizes deformative representations as a "truthful reflection" of a given reality, according to the person or institution engaged in such performances, in line with Bakhtin's (1984) notion of grotesque realism. In other words, the declared intention by the communicator of being fully and disgustingly transparent defines the object of this theory; the aim of "being real" aligns with the aim of challenging established formalities. In this regard, *esperpentic*-performed transparency is strategically viewed as a cost-effective way to achieve a goal (e.g., political or social) by placing the emphasis on its authenticity (Alexander, 2004).

By disrupting the formalities surrounding what is considered the norm or beautiful, grotesque performances reveal all through an "excess of transparency". This is done under the premise of total disclosure, in an environment of exuberant communication that may lead to a paradoxical opacity as a consequence of the "incredible irrationality of information overloads, misinformation, disinformation and out-of-control information" (Lash, 2002, p. 2). We can assimilate this paradox through Tsoukas' (1997) notion of the tyranny of light, used originally to describe the blinding effect of excessive data. In this case, it can be linked to the ocular or performative excesses of an aesthetic of provocation.

This focus on the ocular also highlights the role of affects in the way the public consumes politics or understands current affairs (Citton, 2008; Latour & Lépinay, 2009; Martin-Juchat, 2014). These affects are even more powerful when the audience believes it is observing a performance that could be assimilated with the psychological notion of emotional transparency as "this tendency to overestimate the extent to which others can read one's internal states" (Gilovich, Husted Mesvec & Savitski, 1998, p. 332).

The *esperpento*'s impression of authenticity is paradoxically strengthened by the "exaggeration or magnification of certain traits of a given reality" as a way to covey a "critical realism" (Oliva, 1978, p. 59) (Our translation). The *esperpento* portrays a daily reality that becomes, through deformation, strange and unreal: "the spectator suddenly finds himself in front of a familiar world that surprises and shocks him" (Campanella, 1980, p. 43) (Our translation). Through the double effect of exaggeration and alienation, the *esperpento* achieves its function of social criticism because it defies the conventions and formalities associated with political performance. The ambiguity of grotesque transparency derives from the *esperpento*'s quality of "tragedy that is not tragedy" (Valle-Inclán, 1981, p. 105), easily navigating from one genre to another, from the dramatic to the comedic and vice versa.

The Aquarium Metaphor

The theory of grotesque transparency can be accurately described using the metaphor of the aquarium (see Figure 1.1). The spectators looking at the

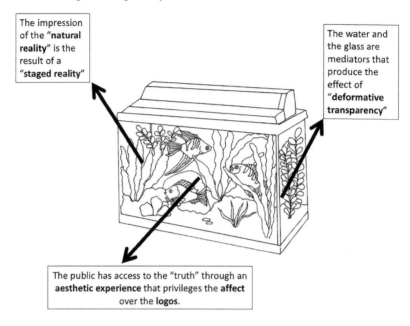

The impression of the "**natural reality**" is the result of a "**staged reality**"

The water and the glass are mediators that produce the effect of "**deformative transparency**"

The public has access to the "truth" through an **aesthetic experience** that privileges the **affect** over the **logos**.

Figure 1.1 The Aquarium Metaphor as Transparent *mise-en-scène*

Source: Isaac Nahon-Serfaty

fish tank believe they are seeing the underwater world as it is. Nevertheless, performed transparency is achieved through the mediation of the glass and the water, both having a deformative effect on the representation and images accessible to the public. Most importantly, the transparency that discloses the underwater world to its audience is the result of a *mise-en-scène*: a well-arranged setting where rocks, plants, and animals are part of a manufactured reality that pretends to be authentic.

Grotesque transparency looks at "ocular politics" as a performance where institutions pretend to convey reality or truth to the public through an act of "total disclosure". By focusing on the aesthetics of deformity— disrupting the canons of acceptability/normality—this form of transparent performance emphasizes affection or passions as the drivers of public communication. The grotesque transparency emphasizes a different kind of reflexivity that underlies the mimetic, the symbolic, and the aesthetic as ways of public deliberation.

The aquarium metaphor also allows us to understand grotesque transparency as a double-way process where the inside and the outside are part of the same system. The strategic performance that occurs inside the aquarium influences and is influenced by the audience's reception of its representation. The transparent degradation staged in the aquarium pretends to have an impact on the perception, attitudes, and eventually behaviour of the public attending the *esperpentic* performance. We can say that the effect (and the affects) caused by the grotesque transparency, which can be measured instantly in digital networks, is feedback that may also reinforce and eventually change the strategy of deformative disclosure. The double-way system of the aquarium metaphor is, however, a mirror that continually reflects social, political, cultural, or economic "realities" outside the fish tank with some kind of distortion, according to Valle-Inclán (1981). In this regard, the mirror or glass becomes a connecting device between the internal representation performed in the aquarium and the external reception conditions of the representation.

The Economy of the Affects

Transparency, as mentioned, can make visible or accessible something that may be considered valuable to someone. But transparency often has unintended consequences. Lord (2006) points out that the value of transparency lies in the information it reveals and the type of behaviour it triggers. A "pragmatics of transparency" explains not only the cognitive gains won from the disclosure of certain truth, but the effects of these revelations. Lord (2006) illustrates her argument with the Rwandan genocide of the 1990s. Community radio stations were transparently disseminating information about the Tutsis' location; the Hutus "empowered" by this information then committed horrible crimes. In this case, the disclosure of truthful information (i.e., the exact location of the Tutsis) was a moral catastrophe. The Hutus who killed the Tutsis in Rwanda saw information about their location as an asset that helped them achieve their genocidal goals. Value here means an empowerment gain received through the revealed information. Value could also be linked, however, to the axiological problem of this knowledge gain's consequences. The question, then, is: where does the value of transparency lie?

I propose to reconcile the notions of value, in the productive or reproductive sense of the term, and values in the ethical sense. Transparency could produce a gain (e.g., financial, political, cultural, social, etc.) but also promote a certain moral vision or an idea of good or acceptable. In his book *La psychologie economique*, Gabriel Tarde (1902/2006) defines value as the result of an intersubjective process:

> It is a quality that we attribute to things, like color, but in reality, as color, exists only in us, of a life that is all subjective. It consists in the agreement of the collective judgments we make about the aptitude of

objects to be more or less, and by a greater or lesser number of persons, raw, desired, or tasted.

(p. 51) (Our translation)

Tarde's (1902/2006) definition emphasizes the role that beliefs, opinions, expectations, and aspirations—as shared ideas or perceptions—contribute to the formation of value. It focuses on the interactive process of assigning value to something or someone that flows from a dynamic of "passionate interests" that often manifests itself in contradictions and public debates (Latour & Lépinay, 2009). In criticizing purely materialistic approaches to value (e.g., Marx's notion of work, the liberal economy approach to the market), Tarde (1902/2006) instead approaches the concept as the result of the "invention potential" of social relations (Lazzarato, 2002). These inter-actions of influence and counter-influence create value (in the reproductive sense) and values (in the axiological sense).

According to Tarde (1902/2006), this intersubjective process produces three types of values: value-truth, value-usefulness, and value-beauty. Value-truth is associated with beliefs and knowledge, or the system of ideas that we accept as valid. Value-usefulness is related to power; the power of law, merit, and wealth that allows access to objects, people, or institutions. Value-beauty focuses on the emotions and sensations that people derive from certain objects, ideas, people, or organizations.

Tarde (1902/2006) establishes a correlation between the truth value and two subsets of values: value-glory and value-credit. These values relate to a person or entity's reputation, but are nourished by different intersubjective dynamics. The value-glory is derived from a certain "halo" that individuals may apply to a person or organization, often related to past achievements or even mythical stories. Value-credit is more so associated with expertise, qualifications, or contributions to society. In his charismatic or productive dimensions, Tarde (1902/2006) in 1902 had already understood the impor-tance of brand image in forming consumer habits and public opinion.

Tarde's (1902/2006) major contribution remains his clear understanding of communication's influence on the creation and reproduction of value through imitative expansion (repetition), opposition (debate and competi-tion), and adoption (consensus/action/consumption). As an example, books illustrate this process of social contagion. Books are a product with a double quality: they are both material and immaterial. Books depend on imitative expansion to succeed (i.e., more readers). They can also create contro-versy or debate that attracts public attention. Finally, books are adopted or accepted as truthful or entertaining because they promote a credible or plau-sible consensual point of view (in fiction, for example). Tarde (1902/2006) also notes that books generate value without losing it. A book can be physically damaged (e.g., become wet or burnt), losing some of its material value. The fundamental value of a book, however, lies in its virtual ability to generate agreement (truth-value), to promote attitudes, behaviours, and abilities (value-usefulness), and to produce affects. In his analysis of books as objects of value, Tarde (1902/2006) anticipates the importance of uses and rewards (Katz, 2006) to explain media consumption and the imitative quality of digital networks.

Whether it is based on the attractiveness of the beautiful or the repulsion of the grotesque, the dominance of the visual in these strategies signifies that the affective dimension is central in the process of institutional communication (Latour & Lépinay, 2009; Martin-Juchat, 2014). Communication is the mechanism of reproduction and expansion in the "society of affects" (Lordon, 2013). Following Citton (2008), the purposeful use of "affect" rather than "feeling" or "emotion" translates the idea that "all affect (*affectus, adfectus*) is an affection (*affectio*), and thus always results [. . .] from an external conditioning" (Citton, 2008, pp. 77–78) (Our translation). These effects are even stronger when the public feels they are witnessing a performance of "total revelation" or "proactive transparency" (Oliver, 2004). In this sense, grotesque transparency becomes a sign of authenticity, as the projected image and performance are perceived as true, supported by the ambiguity of the notion of "aesthetic truth", according to Alexander (2004).

From a strategic point of view, institutions aim to bridge the gap between proclaimed and perceived authenticity (Molleda & Jain, 2013). The institutional objective is to maintain a coherent alignment between their narrative and behaviours. Being perceived as non-authentic, therefore, is a challenge to the organization's reputation and credibility (Molleda, 2010).

In classical terms, the aesthetic experience may be conducive to understanding a truth, or as Umberto Eco (2007) says in his book *On Ugliness*, "those who cultivate the aristocracy of the spirit produce beauty and wisdom" (p. 27). By translating this idea into the terms of strategic communication, an institution creates social value through the emotional shock generated by a deformative or grotesque image of the human body. Paradoxically, the grotesque transparency strategy proposes that value (i.e., cognitive, behavioural, or affective) can be derived from the degraded representation of a dying, sick, or defective body.

Epistemological Boundaries

It is precisely the convergence between the visually grotesque and the impression of transparency that enhances the value of images representing the "realistically true" (worth the pleonasm) more so in its "augmented reality" aspect, in which the edges between the naturally true and the virtually unreal are blurred. There is nothing new in this pretence of grotesque realism (Bakhtin, 1984). Religious art, literature, theatre, and even politics are full of examples of these images, colliding precisely because of their vocation to show the degraded (especially of the human body and other living beings) in its rawest splendour (Carroll, 1990/2004). The novelty now lies in the scope, multiplication, circulation, and manipulation of the grotesquely transparent in a communicational ecology that presents unprecedented social and cultural challenges. The explosion of grotesque transparency puts on the table of social scientists and humanists questions about the consequences of *pantagruelic* production and consumption of transgressive images.

While grotesque transparency manifests itself in a variety of forms and areas, the main argument of this book is that this phenomenon responds to the same unifying logic, even in those manifestations that are described as illegitimate or unjustifiable. As we will discover, grotesque transparency, whether it comes from a legitimate institution such as the World Health Organization or a terrorist network like ISIS, has common features that define a certain organizational rationality and potentially similar psychosocial consequences. The guiding thread that articulates the most absurd manifestations of grotesque transparency goes through an encompassing strategy (understood as the calculation of forces at play and their pragmatics or impact), a disruptive aesthetic (as a sensorial-affective experience), and a problematic ethic (a rupture with moral and even religious schemes).

The cases that will be analysed in this book represent themes and variations of manifestations whose theoretical and practical implications require a multidisciplinary perspective to address their richness and complexity. Although this book could be located in the field of strategic communication, and its derivations within the framework of political and public communication, the mobilization of conceptual and analytical clues from sociology, anthropology, social psychology, philosophy, cultural studies, and even literature are required. It is precisely the fundamentally aesthetic character of grotesque transparency that means we must break away from the rigid schemas of a discipline to account for multiple implications of disruptive visual rhetoric.

However, grotesque transparency overflows the aesthetic considerations, pointing to problems that strategic communication typically considers beyond the limits of its object of study. It reflects the problems that some may encounter when trying to define what "strategy" means in strategic communication (Hallahan et al., 2007). For example, as we will see in the case studies, the revelation of the realistically grotesque in its obscene, degraded, and deformed character forces us to confront the duality of the sacred and the profane in the supposedly secularized public space of modernity. The religious or profane in grotesque transparency, from its disturbing obscurity in Girard's (1972/2010) terms, requires interpretive keys that account for social and cultural processes beyond their functional quantification of how strategies based on visual excesses may affect attitudes and behaviours.

Methodological Notes

From a methodological point of view, this book deals with a variety of phenomenon centred around grotesque transparency in different geographic locations as well as multiple organizational and institutional rationalities that explain and justify it. I do not pretend, however, to have completed an exhaustive inventory of the various ways in which grotesque transparency is expressed. I even believe, as pointed out at the beginning of this chapter, that the strategy of the visually disturbing acquires new and surprising features thanks to an augmented reality that blurs the boundaries between the transparently immediate (physical space) and the transparently virtual (where physical space and digital space converge). The limited sample of cases included in this book is representative of a phenomenon in full expansion, and which assumes facets that the literary imagination can visualize better than any sociological or humanistic study.

All the case studies included in this book belong to the same broad category: they are representative of grotesque transparency strategy. They come from different areas of public life: politics (i.e., Trump and Chávez's populism), terrorism (i.e., ISIS propaganda), and public health (i.e., anti-tobacco and HIV-AIDS prevention). These cases, however, share a common strategic feature. They use a proactive disclosure mechanism that focuses on the diffusion of realistically disturbing visual images and/or performances through digital and analog media. These images and performances represent and employ the out-of-norm or the realistically grotesque (Bakhtin, 1984) as a way to achieve organizational or institutional objectives.

The case studies we will explore illustrate the universality of this shocking strategy, revealing the same motivations and rationality even coming from organizations or institutions with different aims, values, and levels of legitimacy. In politics, terrorist propaganda, or disease prevention, institutions face similar challenges: a highly fragmented media environment, a public pressure for more transparency (i.e., everything should be disclosed), and the preeminence of visual images over the rhetorical or discursive. The transparently grotesque strategy looks to overcome these challenges by justifying that the horrible truth should be conveyed "as is" to do good ("good" being a very relative notion depending on the institutional or organizational source of the strategy).

As in any research, this book follows inclusion and exclusion criteria. The claim of realism made by producers/communicators defines an element of inclusion. The use of fictional realism excludes any manifestations from the definition of grotesque transparency, and thus from our sample of cases.

Each case study has been dissected using a conceptual and interpretative instrument that recognizes the particularities of some representations with a theatrical or performance character and narrative. These representations, while sometimes inverted, break institutional and normative schemes while still emphasizing the visual (i.e., the shocking image). At times, the narratives and performances conveyed through realistically grotesque images (e.g., "authentic", "as is", "direct", "true", etc.) come from organizations considered legitimate, with society accepting them as valid interlocutors telling us what we should think and do. This includes government ministries of health or international organizations, whose missions are to preserve the common good. On other occasions, transparently grotesque representations are used by organizations that have intermediate legitimacy (i.e., organizations that intervene in areas outside their original mission, such as the United Colors of Benetton) and that assume a social cause such as the prevention of HIV-AIDS or the fight against racism. Finally, there are organizations perceived as illegitimate (i.e., terrorist groups) that use the grotesque as a mean to capture the public's attention and achieve propagandistic goals. Even in this category of illegitimate organizations, the very idea of perceived legitimacy is relative, since their actions may be rejected by certain audiences because they are horrible and unworthy; for others, however, their performances and terrible images are legitimate expressions of a struggle that is considered heroic.

The analytical schema used to study these manifestations looks at four dimensions: the ocular (Green, 2010) or shocking/disturbing visual images of the degraded or about-to-be degraded body (Bakhtin, 1984); the performance or social as theatre and *esperpentical* representation (Alexandre, 2004; Valle-Inclán, 1981); aesthetics as the externalization of the economy of affects (Citton, 2008); and, the moral tensions between the sacred and the profane (Girard, 1972/2010) in a logic of desecration or disruption of social values.

The study of images and the staging of what is transparently grotesque must take into account the context of production and reception in which the disruptive strategy gives meaning to a highly emotional or affective communicative process. For example, in the case of anti-smoking campaigns, the disruptive approach is justified by a hygienist rationality to ensure the people's welfare. Showing an image of a dying cancer patient or a person with a hole in their neck on a cigarette package is considered legitimate even if it reaches the limits of what is morally acceptable. In the context of political communication, certain limits are also exceeded either by invoking revolutionary rationality (a rupture with the old order) or strategic rationality to win or lose an election.

The analysis of the grotesquely transparent should also question what happens to the public exposed to these images and performances. Although it is obvious, the study of reception (a term used here on a provisional basis, since it indicates passivity on the public's part) must observe the audience's behaviour and even measure their opinions and attitudes. An initial approach that can be used to investigate this problem is to identify two main potential reactions from the public: an almost visceral rejection of this form of communication, or acceptance of it as a form of identification and projection of certain ideas or worldviews. Between these two poles, there are nuances that a deeper analysis of reception and circulation of the grotesquely transparent will reveal. For now, we can recognize that between the extremes of rejection and acceptance there are intermediate modalities that give strategic meaning to this mode of communication as highly affectively charged, making the mind-body connection clearer to understanding the grotesque transparency strategy.

2 Alternate Reflexivity
The Politics of Excesses

Political scientists face two major challenges. First, they are not clear on how to approach culture as a variable influencing political processes; second, they are not sure how to measure emotions (or affects) and their impact on political decision-making. Obsessed as they are with quantifiable variables, political scientists—particularly those from empirical North American schools—and their peers who study political communication often miss the qualitative importance of culture and emotions in politics. That's why Régis Debray suggested that we need a "politics of affection" to fully capture what happens in political processes (1981, p. 187). Otherwise, political scientists and political communication scholars may take the path of least resistance by simply dismissing and tagging social processes as manifestations of populism, "irrational politics", or even as some kind of "backwardness."

While it is clear that support for populism has returned, based on recent trends observed across the political spectrum including the far left and the far right, I argue that its grotesque manifestations are more than demagoguery and affective manipulations of voters and partisans. The strategy of grotesque transparency can reveal not only the character of a politician or a political organization, but also convey the state of the "politics of affection" in a given society. Returning to the metaphor of the aquarium (see Chapter 1), the use of the visually disgusting, disturbing, or out-of-the-norm as part of a strategic political endeavour makes a statement about both the political body involved and the public watching the performance.

The use of grotesque strategy in political communication is symptomatic of the tension between tradition and modernity. In Western countries and some other westernized societies, we live under the illusion that the adoption of formal democratic rituals and economic progress has weakened the importance of mythical discourses. It is clear, however, that recent disruptive social and political events have marked a powerful return of the myth to the public sphere. Perhaps the most powerful of these was the election of

Barack Obama as president of the United States of America in 2008. With Obama's successful bid for the White House, the "politics of affection" reached its peak—not only because the U.S. elected its first black president, but primarily because the public perceived it as an important social and cultural breakthrough.

Beyond its political significance, the election of Obama—as with the 1998 election of Hugo Chávez in Venezuela or the most recent American election of Donald Trump—was driven and triggered by processes that can be explained through the lenses of aesthetical reflexivity (Lash, 2002), as sense-making and identity-building mechanisms introduced by neo-mythical discourses in the context of a fragmented, global Babel (Nahon-Serfaty, 2010). Without denying the relevance of the political and economic calculations behind these phenomena, I will argue in this chapter that the "politics of visual excesses", particularly in the cases of Chávez and Trump, played a pivotal role in their elections and their performances as presidents.

According to philosopher Yeshayahu Leibowitz (1995), "people" is not an objective entity but the product of a subjective reality. People, in this sense, are the result of a historical consciousness transmitted from generation to generation as well as a national subjectivity. This subjectivity is the crystallization of a long accumulation of representations, mindsets, and discourses that provide a sense-making framework. At the heart of this national subjectivity is myth, the narrative structure that articulates a collective memory and projects its collective future. Myth has the particularity of being tri-temporal, given that it can connect the past with the future, and especially, make sense of the present. Its narrative efficacy comes from this circular quality of an almost perfect internal coherence. Like religious dogma, myth provides a total explanatory system for the world. Myth and dogma are both discursive platforms that serve political and spiritual powers, shaping collective subjectivity and framing collective action.

An analysis of grotesque transparency situates the neo-myth in the context of global communication networks and hyper-information. From a pragmatic perspective, the main question that confronts us is how the expression and reception of such visual rhetoric are influenced by the dynamics of globalization. I will also explore how the strategic diffusion of grotesque images works as a meaning-production mechanism in societies with highly fragmented discourses and where there are difficulties building consensual views. Finally, this book will examine the ethical consequences that emerge from the political uses and abuses of deformative transparency as a polarizing political strategy. Before answering these questions and analysing the case studies to illustrate the politics of excesses, I will explore the relationship between strategic communication, disruption, and order.

Between Chaos and Control

Strategic communication, at its essence, is about control. Rather than the illusion of a public sphere where rational citizens engage in communicative deliberation (Habermas, 1993) or symmetrical, horizontal two-way communication (Grunig, Grunig & Dozier, 2009), Bernays (1928/2005), the father of modern propaganda, explained it clearly when he defined "Public Relations" (PR):

> The conscious and intelligent manipulation of the organized habits and opinions of the masses is an important element in democratic society. Those who manipulate this unseen mechanism of society constitute an invisible government which is the true ruling power of our country.
>
> (p. 9)

For Bernays (1928/2005), strategy meant "organizing chaos" to contain society's tendency towards violence and conflict. In this regard, the pioneer of modern PR shared the pessimism of his uncle Sigmund Freud, who in *Civilization and Its Discontents* (1930/1955) stated:

> But perhaps we shall also accustom ourselves to the idea that there are certain difficulties inherent in the very nature of culture which will not yield to any efforts at reform. Over and above the obligations of putting restrictions upon our instincts, which we see to be inevitable, we are imminently threatened with the dangers of a state one may call "*la misere psychologique*" of groups. This danger is most menacing where the social forces of cohesion consist predominantly of identifications of the individuals in the group with one another, whilst leading personalities fail to acquire the significance that should fall to them in the process of group-formation.
>
> (p. 106) (Our translation)

Freud's (1930/1955) point of view was influenced by Gustave Le Bon's (1905/2001) study of the psychology of the crowd, which he described as an entity marked by impulsiveness and irritability, and which was easily suggestible, emotionally driven, and intolerant. Spanish philosopher Ortega y Gasset (1929/2012) was also critical of both the masses and the mass-men ("*hombres masa*") of whom they are made up, contrasting "noble life" and "common life" and excoriating the barbarism and primitivism he saw in the mass-men.

The collective's *misere psychologique* (either as a crowd or mass) is the basis for the duality of all political communication between disruption and order. Hitler and Lenin understood this very well. Bolshevik propaganda had a dual function of "political revelation" (or denunciation), which was meant to be highly disruptive of the established order while also guiding in a new order by using slogans or watchwords to present simplified versions of reality (Domenach, 1979). The Nazis also made the differentiation between the "brutal persuasion" of the majority, leveraging its natural *pulsions* (Tchakhotine, 1992), and the more rational persuasion of the illustrated minority that were considered as influencers.

Whether operating from an organizing or disorganizing perspective, strategic political communication translates the guiding principles of war into the civil realm. This is why, for example, strategic political communication centres around "campaigns" (i.e., a connected series of military or civilian operations designed to bring about a particular result). This is also why we associate campaigning with power preservation or control and the diffusion of a doctrine (i.e., an ideological "truth"). From a topological point of view, strategic campaigning means to conquer a privileged position (in military terms, a "high place") from where you can manipulate the forces in the social and psychological fields. In effect, the grotesque transparency strategy claims that by promoting chaos or disruption, an individual or organization can achieve a political goal. Whoever uses this approach is, in the spirit of Lenin, prioritizing the revelation or total disclosure of a disgusting, disturbing, or unsettling visual truth as a legitimate means to conquer or preserve power.

Before moving forward with the case studies, we will touch briefly on the master of all political communicators, Machiavelli (Machiavel, 2009). Well before the era of ocular politics (Green, 2010) and socially performed representations (Alexander, 2004), the Florentine politician provided a conceptual framework for the strategic importance of image management in politics. Projecting a certain image that could be modulated *ad necessitas* from "being" merciful, humane, and religious to "being" cruel or inhumane—depending on the political leader's goals—was the amoral skill required to keep order and avoid violence. According to Machiavelli (Machiavel, 2009, 2013), the strategic objective of keeping power was more critical, and subsequently more amoral, than the ethical imperatives of the common good. Performing these qualities, however—even if the political leader cannot truly possess them—maintains the peace of his domain.

The visual, therefore, overcomes the discursive because "men, *in universali*, judge more with their eyes that their hands, since each one can easily see but understands very little" (Machiavel, 2009, pp. 109–110, Our translation). As noted by Schill (2012, p. 122), visual images play many functions in political communication as a way to reinforce arguments, set agendas, and dramatize policy, but also to connect to societal symbols and even add ambiguity.

Disclosure and Denunciation

There are many cases that can be used to illustrate the validity of the grotesque transparency approach in studying political communication. They come from different political traditions and contexts, demonstrating the universality of a phenomenon shaped by several factors including the emergence of a populism with neo-mythical traits, the expansion of digital networks (with their emphasis on the global circulation of visual images), and the pressure for more transparency, even if transparency means public disclosure of the degraded, horrible, or shocking.

I will start by looking at Hugo Chávez's "media presidency" (Cañizález, 2012, p. 62), and in particular, two exceptional moments during his long tenure as *Comandante* of the so-called Bolivarian revolution in Venezuela. The first of these took place on July 15, 2010, in the middle of the night. Via Twitter, Chávez announced that the remains of Simón Bolívar, the liberator of five South American nations, had been exhumed to find the "true cause" of his death more than 200 years ago. A few hours later, a video showing the opening of the sarcophagus containing Bolívar's skeleton was broadcast on all of the country's television channels. The second moment occurred on Holy Thursday, April 5, 2012, when Chávez spoke during the mass in his hometown of Sabaneta de Barinas. This event, broadcast on national television and radio, was especially dramatic because Chávez was suffering from terminal cancer and used the occasion to plead for his health in a confessional tone.

The other case studies I will analyse fall within two different political contexts and orientations. They are representative of a North American, right-wing populism and are exemplary illustrations of a strategy of denunciation, in contrast to the strategy of revelation we will see with Chávez. One of these case studies is the video of former Toronto mayor Rob Ford smoking crack, which was originally released in 2013. The other is the video of Donald Trump, then-host of *The Apprentice*, making remarks about the female body and the way he treated women. This latter video was originally recorded in 2005 but released during the U.S. presidential campaign in 2016.

I would like to make an important clarification before moving forward with the case studies. In political communication, a strategy of denunciation can be seen as a move towards full disclosure of a certain situation or issue, which alerts the public and its institutions about improper behaviour by an elected official or an individual vying to be elected. A strategy of revelation, meanwhile, is a conscious and planned disclosure by a political leader or organization, done to achieve a goal by creating the impression of total transparency.

Chávez's Affective Transparency

Previously, the discourse of Hugo Chávez has been studied as a form of mythical rhetoric with epic connotations that attempted to consolidate a political identity (Capriles, 2006; Nahón -Serfaty, 2010; Torres, 2009). This discourse, characterized by a narrative of emancipation, is highly persuasive because it resonates with imaginaries that are engrained in the mindset of Venezuelan society and which embody the syncretism of the European, Hispano-Catholic, and Aboriginal mentalities (Briceño Guerrero, 1997). In addition, Chávez's discourse has strong messianic connotations, with elements of traditional Catholic theology merging with unorthodox popular religiosity (Peraza, 2013). The objective of this book, however, is to explore an alternative path to interpreting this discourse as a political representation from the point of view of aesthetical reflexivity (Lash, 1995), through the analytical lenses of grotesque transparency. I argue that this performance corresponds more to the *esperpento*—as defined by Valle-Inclán (1981)—than the mythical epic.

Before completing an analysis of Chávez's performances, we will explore the context in which the now-deceased president implemented his strategy of revelation. This description will be guided by the following question: is there anything about the so-called Bolivarian revolution that was different from the typical militaristic and caudillo-centric regimes that dominated Venezuelan republican history? One could be tempted to answer that nothing is new in this context, which resurrects the well-known atavistic cult of Bolivar and the strongman in addition to a mix of populist politics nourished by the petro-state's wealth (Coronil, 1997). Historian Carreras Damas (2011) has qualified *chavismo* as the most recent manifestation of the Bolivarianism-militarism (*bolivarianismo-militarismo*), which he describes as an "ideology of replacement" for liberal and social-democratic political programs.

Nevertheless, some authors have identified new characteristics in the *chavista* era. Pino Iturrieta (2013) notes the main contrast with past socio-political processes resides in the capability of this regime—even after Chávez's passing—to change individuals' routines through a system that strongly "influence[s] the private life and the collective attitudes" (pp. 16–17). Bisbal (2009, 2013), meanwhile, has studied the consolidation of a "communicational hegemony" in the last 19 years, when the state became "the space-mechanism of intervention in the life of society and, thus . . . an agent of intervention and regulation of different and diverse realities involved in society" (p. 49, Our translation).

This era was defined by the invasive nature of Chávez's media performances via his weekly show *Aló Presidente* and the long national broadcasts known as *cadenas* that demonstrated the political dynamics at play in Venezuela (Morales, 2013; Rosa Gualda, 2012). According to Cañizález (2012), Chávez's "media presidency" (*presidencia mediática*) (p. 62) was not only a large and sophisticated propaganda machine, but was literally a media-based government where policy and decision-making were performed live on television (Chirinos, 2013). Culturally, the *chavista* regime also displaced the former elites by creating and consolidating institutions (e.g., museums, film production facilities and grants, publishing corporations, etc.) that served the interests of the revolution, claiming it was being done to defend popular culture (*cultura popular*) and the "true" national identity (Kozak Rovero, 2013; Silva-Ferrer, 2013).

Beyond the controversy regarding the theses of continuity versus rupture, the *chavista* regime clearly built a new communicational and symbolic ecosystem that survived the physical absence of its leader, Hugo Chávez. What is new here is not the well-known and documented rhetoric of the "good revolutionary" (*buen revolucionario*) (Rangel, 1976/2005), but the sophisticated and expansive network of media, discourses, and images that shape individuals' subjectivity. It could be argued this hegemonic aim is not novel, given that it plays the same dominant role as the propaganda apparatuses of communism and fascism; however, as will be illustrated in this book's analysis, Chávez's case represents a powerful combination of atavistic imaginaries and the tools of a hyper-connected world.

Chávez as Serpent-Charmer

Chávez's Twitter announcement on July 15, 2010, and the subsequent televised exhumation of Simón Bolívar's remains (see Figure 2.1), would be in principle an expression of institutional transparency, done to inform the public about a process involving the hero par excellence of Venezuelan history. From a formal point of view, this gesture would appear at first reading to be transparent. But this performance also followed a strategy of hyper-mediatization of institutional action (Bisbal, 2009), centred on the constant presence of the *Comandante Supremo* of the Bolivarian Revolution on television screens and radio waves. Chávez's strategy was that of hyper-visibility saturation, which makes it necessary to ask to what extent this saturation would have a contrary effect and create opacity (Reyna, 2013).

Nevertheless, this public display of a hero's remains aligns with political communication that focuses on reconfiguring national myth (Nahón-Serfaty, 2010; Torres, 2009). This type of communication seeks to draw a parallel between the founding hero (Bolívar) and the contemporary hero (Chávez). Here, the drive for transparency comes from a desire for rapprochement between the two hero characters. It is not an insignificant detail

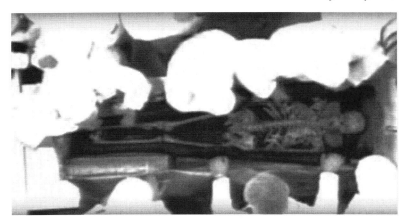

Figure 2.1 The Skeleton of Simón Bolívar during the Exhumation as Shown on National TV

Source: Image capture from video of the Venezuelan Ministry of Information and Communication available on YouTube

to note that Chávez's voiceover accompanies the first scattered images of the ritual stripping of Bolívar's corpse.

From the point of view of a pragmatics of communication, the effect of rapprochement between these characters is less important than the effect of the hero's desacralization. Bolívar's traditional iconography is one of a hero on horseback during the War of Independence, the wise legislator who drafted the constitutions of the emerging South American states, or even the almost-mystical image of his delirium on the Chimborazo pike where he imagined one unified Latin American country. In all these representations, there are elements of a republican religion (Pino Iturrieta, 2003) in which the "divine" Bolívar plays the role of major god in a pantheon of military heroes (Torres, 2009). To show *urbi et orbi* his remains—the skeleton of the Father of the fatherland—has precisely the effect described by Valle-Inclán (1981) in his characterization of the *esperpento*; namely, the distortion of the hero's image by the concave mirrors. We are no longer in the epic register, given that transparent access to the hero's mortal image in his real state produces an upheaval in the public's imagination.

In a speech that preceded the exhumation video, Chávez addressed the rumours spread by his political opposition about the witchcraft supposedly being practiced with the Liberator's bones by him and his relatives. Even after disqualifying these "sick" rumours, Chávez echoed the opinions of part of the Venezuelan public who saw in this ritual the grotesque action of a regime that had gone too far—a "profaner of burials" and "heretics" who had "opened the door to Bolívar's curse". In this case, transparency is grotesque because of an image that is not necessarily absurd but certainly distorted. The image of Bolívar's skeleton contradicts the expectations of a part of the audience who would have preferred the social imaginary representation of the god in Olympus (Darias Príncipe, 1996).

The aesthetic reading of this act as distorting transparency must also turn to the rather kitschy side of a ritual that contains all the ingredients for a typical military staging: soldiers who salute the superior, the national anthem, and the flag, in addition to white suits and masks that add a touch of science fiction. In the face of these images, we find ourselves between the hyperrealism of kitsch, which situates us in the commonplace of patriotic rhetoric, and the unrealistic and unthinkable, specifically in the desacralization of the fatherland's founder. Thus, we return to Campanella's (1980) observation on the *esperpento*, in that the audience is destabilized by the surprise of an extreme act.

This rhetoric of deforming transparency has an openly religious tone. The hero, even in the grotesque image of his remains being shown to the public, is a supernatural being and the state (the army included) becomes the church of a patriotic cult. It should be noted that this mythical discourse also sometimes includes Christian references, as will be demonstrated in analysing Chávez's next performance.

Is this an act of provocation from a propaganda strategy or a reconfiguration of the social imaginary through a desecration of the nation's institutions? The *esperpento*'s critical function is expressed here by a double communicative game. On one hand, the propagandist stratagem confirms its effectiveness, as the charismatic leader (Chávez)—by an almost *thaumaturgical* act—attracts and maintains society's attention. On the other hand, the objective of the social imaginary's reconfiguration is manifested in the actions that followed the exhumation; specifically, the presentation of Bolívar's "real" face, which was reconstituted numerically from the remains of the publicly revealed skull (as seen in Figure 2.2). Once again, we are faced with a quest for transparency through an artifice (i.e., the digital image of Bolívar) that seeks to supplant traditional iconography that is much less "realistic" than the computer recreation of his face.

These actions, however, cannot be analysed as only a desire to reconstruct the past in order to shape the collective memory. Using the notion of "invented tradition" introduced by Hobsbawm and Ranger (1983), the rhetoric of deforming transparency seeks to rewrite history in order to justify and legitimize the actions of the "new state". The historical authenticity of the invented traditions invoked by this rhetoric is often problematic, though their value does not lie in their veracity. Instead, they are a source of meaning used to connect the mythical past and the actuality. The struggle for Venezuelan independence is a historic fact. The invented tradition,

Figure 2.2 Hugo Chávez Presenting on National TV the Digitally Reconstituted "True" Face of Simón Bolívar

Source: Image capture from a video of the Venezuelan Ministry of Information and Communication available on YouTube

however, claims there was continuity between emancipation processes led by different actors at different times in the country's history.

Invented traditions are much more than mere intellectual creations used to build a historical argument. They are, as Hobsbawm and Ranger (1983) show, ritual and spectacle. The mythical narrative is a staging that captures the people's imagination. Invented traditions are deployed in rituals that multiply, especially military rituals, and in the consolidation of a new patriotic calendar. In fact, the effectiveness of these traditions depends less on their argumentative coherence than on the discourse's narrative quality and the persuasive power of certain images. Tradition has a certain resonance in the collective imagination because this discourse shares a similar code to melodrama and telenovela, television genres well-anchored in the Latin American social imagination.

Chávez's second performance took place on April 5, 2012, when he appeared on national television during the *Jueves Santo* (Holy Thursday) mass, again being celebrated in his hometown (see Figure 2.3). This mass was dedicated to Chávez's health, as he was suffering from what we now know was terminal cancer, and included a short homily by a priest. When the priest was about to close the ceremony by asking the parishioners to "leave in peace" ("*pueden ir en paz*"), Chávez interrupted him and moved to the front to say "a few words". His speech lasted approximately 45 minutes, with Chávez playing the homiletic role usually reserved for the priest. Even though his words had a deeply personal and emotional connotation

Figure 2.3 Hugo Chávez During the Holy Thursday Mass; behind Him Is the Image of *Jesús el Nazareno*

Source: Image capture from a video of the Venezuelan Ministry of Information and Communication available on YouTube

(his parents and siblings were at the mass), he also made remarks that may qualify as an unorthodox theology (see box entitled *Emotional revelations*).

This analysis will focus on Chávez's speech, the actors (e.g., Chávez, members of his family and particularly his mother, the priest, and the audience present at the mass), and the broadcast images, all of which became constitutive elements of his performance in a televised *mise-en-scène*. Typically, Chávez's presentations were both improvised (he rarely read his speeches) and well-scripted. Analytically, we will look at a "script" that, according to Alexander (2006), reveals the friction between "background representations" (i.e., socio-cultural and even political collective representations) and the contingency of live, televised performance (p. 58). We will then dissect this performance using the grotesque transparency framework, focusing on its *esperpentic* character. In this case, Chávez functions as the centre of a paradigmatic performance of the dying hero, who becomes an expression of the exceptional, the extreme, and the highly dramatic. This chapter will also demonstrate how he disrupted established formalities and the meanings behind symbols and rituals that support background representations.

During the entire Holy Thursday broadcast, Chávez stood in front of an image of *Jesús el Nazareno*, the representation of a suffering Christ carrying the cross and wearing a purple garment. During parts of Chávez's speech, the broadcast's director zoomed the camera out from the Nazareno's face, which in the image was bleeding from the crown of thorns he wore. The president, meanwhile, was wearing a rosary around his neck.

The *esperpentic* feature of this particular performance clearly illustrates one premise of grotesque transparency: it renders visible a side of the hero that is normally hidden or minimized by the mythical narrative. In this sense, the performance corresponds to the notion of "grotesque realism" (Bakhtin, 1984), which transitions the ideal to the material and which was represented by Chávez via his sick body. As per Valle-Inclán (1981), the classical hero's image becomes distorted through mediation by the glass or mirror (the medium), exhibiting ugliness or weaknesses that are usually hidden by the hero's extraordinary accomplishments. In this mass performance, Chávez— the heroic *Comandante* of the Bolivarian Revolution—disclosed his emotional frailty and fears regarding his disease. In this mediated performance, the hero becomes deformed by the concave mirrors and loses his "immaculate attributes". By doing so, however, he can strategically close the gap between claimed and perceived authenticity (Molleda & Jain, 2013) and reinforce the connection with his followers, who are emotionally attached to their leader and his revolution (Lecumberri, 2012).

This kind of deformative transparency creates the illusion of total disclosure, in particular a sentimental disclosure where feelings are conveyed with the brutal honesty of dramatic circumstances (i.e., Chávez facing a terminal disease). This performance showcases the tensions that exist between the transparency of showing everything and the opacity that surrounded his diagnosis, treatment, convalescence, and finally, his passing.

Chávez's performance, including his use of religious images, also meets the "critical realism" function of the *esperpento*. In this case, criticism manifested through the displacement of the sacred (i.e., the public exhumation of Bolívar's remains). Chávez also visually displaced Christ from the centre of the mass, putting himself in front of the scene and placing the *Nazareno* in the back, which was especially problematic in the context of the Holy Thursday celebration. In addition, through his homiletic exercise, Chávez desecrated this ritual further by introducing his personal theological arguments, such as equating Ché Guevara and Jesus on the same level of Christology.

The narrative of the *Comandante*, while not necessarily linear or well-structured, is also *esperpentic* because it flows easily from personal drama to the banality of a silly joke. Rhetorically effective, this hybrid discourse moves from the supposedly sublime to the mundane, breaking the limits between genres (i.e., the presidential speech or the homily) and normative frameworks (i.e., breaking the ritual's sequence). The sacred becomes fluid and comprehensive, losing the qualities that makes it "uniquely pure from an ethical point of view" (Tessier & Prades, 1991, p. 21). Chávez's irreverent narrative resonated with the Venezuelan religious syncretism, where the sacred and profane coexist in various manifestations of popular religiosity (Ascencio, 2012). More importantly, this "charismatic domination transforms all values and breaks all traditional and rational norms" (Weber, 1978, p. 1115), appealing to the revolutionary imagery of the charismatic community (i.e., the people). In this context, the aquarium metaphor proves its heuristic value as a double-way process where the performer and spectators influence each other based on common cultural and social ground.

Emotional Revelations

Hugo Chávez's performance during the Holy Thursday of April 2012 (Chávez, 2012) was "emotionally transparent". His initial remarks were about memories of his youth and references to his feelings while he was holding "the loving hand of my mother, the loving hand of my father" ("*la mano de mi madre amorosa, la mano amorosa de mi padre*"). He justified his words that day because of his urgent need of opening up in a confessional tone:

> because sometimes one feels many things that usually don't say, but today I feel the need—Father (referring to the priest)—of saying what I've been feeling for almost a year, when I started to assume that I have inside of me a very malign disease, and as we know is a real menace that marks the end of the road for many people, the end of the physical road. This is the truth

The "emotional transparency" achieved its peak towards the end of the speech. A tearful Chávez implored to be cured of his cancer:

> if all what one has lived hasn't been enough, is what I feel, and I tell God, if what one lived and has lived hasn't been enough, that I deserved this, I welcome it, but give me life, even if it's burning life, painful life, I don't care [. . .] (applause). Give me your crown Christ! Give it to me that I am ready to bleed! Give me your cross, a hundred of crosses that I carry them, but give me life because I still have things to do for this people and for this Fatherland [. . .] (Applause). Don't take me yet, give me your cross, give me your thorns, give me your blood, I am ready to carry them but with life, Christ my Lord. Amen

Between the dramatic highs at the beginning and towards the end of his speech, Chávez made a few jokes about his family and himself—a common feature in his public presentations—that contributed to create the sensation of an "emotional rollercoaster". He engaged in a dialogue with his mom (Elena) about the wooing stratagems of his father:

> President Chávez: Where my father wooed you? In San Hipólito? Well! Elena Frías de Chávez: My dear, God bless you, protects you [. . .] President Chávez: Let's not talk about that, secret

Later in the performance, after talking about the validity of Darwin's evolution theory (that according to Chávez was accepted by Pope John Paul II), he made the following remarks:

> In truthfulness, we come from the monkey. The genetic difference between a monkey and us is 0.2 per cent, or even less, pay attention to the monkey. Recently I saw a monkey, he was dancing, and when he sees a girl he dances, dances, he is in love that monkey, Ah! (Laughs) The monkey in love

In a more serious and solemn note, Chávez also used some of his typical rhetorical "tricks" making a parallelism in his narrative among Bolivar, Christ, and some other revolutionary figures, including himself. Chávez presented the narrative of the "parallel lives" of the heroes:

> Since I was a kid already my life was not mine [. . .] And it has been like this all these years. And I remembered Bolivar, Bolivar when he said in Angostura: "I've been only a simple toy dragged by the revolutionary hurricane [. . .]" this life has been in truthfulness like this. And remembering Bolivar, and looking at the image of the Christ Nazareno with his Cross, with his crown of thorns, with his blood, in his Calvary, in his passion, I remembered that Bolivar also said, certainly when he actually met with Christ

Here Chávez lost track of the speech for a moment and diverted to another subject, to come back later to complete Bolivar's remark about him, Christ, and Don Quixote "the three great idiots—*majaderos*—in history".

The homiletic character of the performance became evident when Chávez entered the unorthodox path of his particular "revolutionary theology". He compared, for example, Che Guevara with Christ:

> Che Guevara, another Christ who lived and died as Christ; like Bolivar he lived and died *"crísticamente"*, not even *"cristiana-mente"*, *"crísticamente"*!. The Che

He also reflected on the "socialist" doctrine of Jesus, conveying an argument that is close to the one advanced by the Liberation Theology (Gutiérrez, 1971):

> I say that with Christ ideas, the ideas of Jesus, we can develop the foundations of a socialist project. I said once that Christ was socialist. A Catholic bishop responded here: "This is not possible, that it was like saying that Christ was an airplane pilot [. . .]". And not only Christ, all the great prophets of Christianity, Isaiah. Oh Isaiah! Isaiah was a whip

Death is the underlying topic of this performance, even when is not being openly named. But at some point, Chávez referred to death in a sort of superstitious invocation or counter-invocation:

> One day he said to me (referring to his mentor General Pérez Arcaya): "I am listening to you, to your speeches, and you are talking too much about death. You shouldn't, because abyssus abyssus invocate". He threw to me a *latinazo*: "The abyss calls the abyss." Thus one should feel and talk about life, love, hope [. . .] even in the difficult circumstances of life

Trump and Ford: Grotesque Revelations

The case studies of Donald Trump during the 2016 presidential campaign and Rob Ford during his tenure as mayor of Toronto are representative of another kind of grotesque transparency that can be called "strategic revelation". It is clear that in both cases, the main objective behind the public disclosures was to denounce their corrupt behaviours, with one running to become a public official (Trump) and the other already elected (Ford). In communication, however, a strategy's outcomes are not always guaranteed. In the case of Trump's *esperpentic* revelation in the 2005 video[1] (see Figure 2.4), his grotesque remarks about the female body and the way

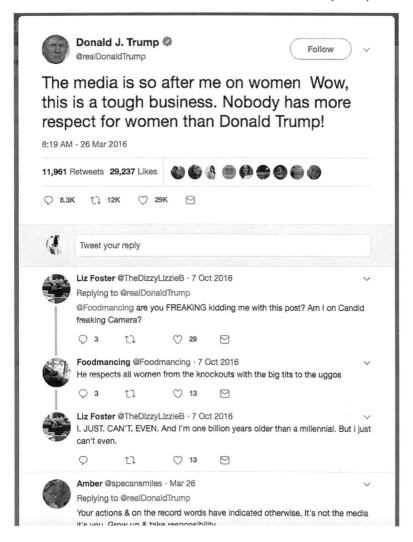

Figure 2.4 Donald Trump's Tweet after the Public Disclosure of the Access Hollywood Video

Source: Image: Video capture from Twitter

he treated women (read excerpts of the video in the box *The talk*) did not impact the support he received from some women voters, particularly white women who favoured Trump over Clinton (52–45 per cent). According to *New Republic*, a liberal website, "it seems that all the talk about Trump's treatment of women turning women voters away from him may have just been some wishful thinking" (Hong, 2016, par. 3).

The Talk

Excerpts of the conversation between Donald Trump (at the time host of the show *The Apprentice*), Billy Bush (at the time host of the show *Access Hollywood*), and Arianne Zucker (actress) (Bullock, 2016):

TRUMP: Yeah, that's her. With the gold. I better use some Tic Tacs just in case I start kissing her. You know, I'm automatically attracted to beautiful—I just start kissing them. It's like a magnet. Just kiss. I don't even wait. And when you're a star, they let you do it. You can do anything.

BUSH: Whatever you want.

TRUMP: Grab 'em by the pussy. You can do anything.

BUSH: Uh, yeah, those legs, all I can see is the legs.

TRUMP: Oh, it looks good.

BUSH: Come on shorty.

TRUMP: Ooh, nice legs, huh?

BUSH: Down below, pull the handle.

TRUMP: Hello, how are you? Hi!

ARIANNE ZUCKER: Hi, Mr. Trump. How are you? Pleasure to meet you.

TRUMP: Nice seeing you. Terrific, terrific. You know Billy Bush?

BUSH: Hello, nice to see you. How you doing, Arianne?

ZUCKER: Doing very well, thank you. Are you ready to be a soap star?

TRUMP: We're ready, let's go. Make me a soap star.

BUSH: How about a little hug for the Donald? He just got off the bus.

ZUCKER: Would you like a little hug, darling?

TRUMP: O.K., absolutely. Melania said this was O.K.

BUSH: How about a little hug for the Bushy? I just got off the bus.

ZUCKER: Bushy, Bushy.

BUSH: Here we go. Excellent. Well, you've got a nice co-star here.

ZUCKER: Yes, absolutely.

TRUMP: Good. After you.

[Break in video]

TRUMP: Come on, Billy, don't be shy.

BUSH: Soon as a beautiful woman shows up, he just, he takes off. This always happens.

TRUMP: Get over here, Billy.

ZUCKER: I'm sorry, come here.

BUSH: Let the little guy in here, come on.

ZUCKER: Yeah, let the little guy in. How you feel now? Better? I should actually be in the middle.

BUSH: It's hard to walk next to a guy like this.
ZUCKER: Here, wait, hold on.
BUSH: Yeah, you get in the middle, there we go.
TRUMP: Good, that's better.
ZUCKER: This is much better. This is —
TRUMP: That's better. . .

Figure 2.5 Rob Ford Smoking Crack
Source: Video capture released by the Toronto Police

In the case study of then-mayor Rob Ford (see Figure 2.5), the revelation's outcomes were different but still demonstrated the limits of transparent grotesque strategy. Ford consistently denied the existence of a video and that he had used crack cocaine, and remained mayor even though several members of Toronto City Council as well as the editorial boards of the *National Post*, the *Toronto Sun*, and the *Toronto Star* called for him to step down. Even after police confirmed the existence of a video showing the mayor smoking crack and making homophobic and racist remarks, Ford announced he would not resign from office. Even more interestingly, after the police announcement about the video, Ford's approval rating rose slightly from 39 to 44 per cent (Alamenciak, 2013).

Trump and Ford's revelations illustrate the complexity of grotesque transparency reception. The public reacts to the grotesque in different ways; sometimes this is done with laughter or by imposing a critical distance towards the *esperpentic*. Other times, the public is horrified, or prefers to remain in a state of denial and not to see it at all.

Returning to the aquarium metaphor as an example of two-way performative dynamics, it becomes clear there is a reinforcing process that occurs between the performer of the grotesque act and their spectators. The well-established North American ritual of public confession confirms this. Many public figures, athletes, politicians, and actors have engaged in the act of a public confession. The confession itself has a more or less standard format; the confessor stands in front of a camera and admits to their sin with a regretful expression. Some are more cynical than others (e.g., Bill Clinton affirming he did not have sexual relations with Monica Lewinsky, or Trump's non-apology for his degrading remarks about women), but in the end, each seeks absolution or public understanding through this ritual.

More recently, a new element has been added to the act of public confession: the perpetrator announcing that they suffer from an addiction and will be admitted to a specialized health center to treat the "disorder" in question. Ford, and more recently Harvey Weinstein, both had to "acknowledge" that they needed help dealing with their respective addictions (drugs and alcohol in one case, sex in the other). The confessions of these public figures reinforced the idea that they were also "victims" of disorders they could not control, and sought sympathy from the public (in some case, this sympathy is indeed received, as with Ford). In addition, their confessional rituals provided them with an "alibi"—likely following the advice of lawyers and public relations consultants—so that a judge may eventually consider mental insanity as an extenuating factor in their crimes.

The ingredients that feed the entertaining and spectacular side of these scandals make them even more grotesque. Valle-Inclán (1981) would undoubtedly have ample material from these case studies to write new plays with decadent characters and moralizing satire. As in all theatrical performances, however, we are yet again faced with a two-way system: what you see and who is seeing it. Sometimes, the public is more understanding and complacent in response to these situations, especially in front of the powerful (Trump can say so). On other occasions, the audience is more severe in their judgments. The public's values are also deformative and relatively elastic, much like the image of the hero that is projected in the *esperpento*'s concave mirrors.

The Aesthetics of Spectacular Politics

The key motivation driving a transparently grotesque strategy is the principle that the truth should always be disclosed to the public, even is that truth is shocking, horrific, or awful. In a reversal of classical reasoning, aesthetics is the vehicle towards the truth, but through the excessive and deformative rather than the beautiful. Even so, the revelation-denunciation motivation may produce contradictory results. On one hand, as noted by Zaretsky (2017b), the transparently grotesque shows how the "long dismissed as a fool" (following Bakhtin's (1984) interpretation of the carnivalesque) is or was crowned king (or president in Trump's case, or mayor in Ford's). On the other hand, the disclosure of the grotesque reinforces the idea among certain audience members that they are witnessing a performance of authenticity (Molleda, 2010), which is a defining element of populism and polarizing politics.

The distinctiveness of these *esperpentic* performances, and perhaps their appeal, resides in their similarities to other forms of entertainment such as reality television (Andacht, 2010), and in the case of Hugo Chávez, the melodrama or telenovelas that are linked to Latin American culture and politics (Acosta-Alzuru, 2014; Acosta-Alzuru, 2011). Jorge Luis Borges (1955/2011), for example, defined Perón's regime in Argentina—a regime that shared many similarities with Chávez's Bolivarian revolution—as *l'illusion comique*, "where the methods of commercial propaganda and literature for concierges were applied to the government of the republic" (p. 9, Our translation).

As we have seen with these case studies, culture informs strategy and contributes to enriching the often-rigid "rational" analytics of political communication. Culture also has an anticipatory function in political phenomena. In his observations about the birth of Evita Perón's myth and the role that literature played in her "mythification", Argentinian writer Tomás Eloy Martínez (1996) observed:

> The fascination for the dead body [of Evita] began even before the disease, in 1950. That year, Julio Cortázar finished *El examen*, a novel impossible to publish in more than one way, as he himself declared it in the prologue of three decades later. It is the story of an animal crowd that comes from all corners of Argentina to worship a bone in the Plaza de Mayo. The crowd is waiting for some kind of miracle, their souls are broken by a woman dressed in white, "very disheveled blond hair falling down to her breasts". She is good, She is very good, they repeat, the little black heads that invade the city, transfiguring themselves into fungi and poisoned mists. The terror that floats in the air is not the terror of Perón but of Her, that from the immortal bottom of history drags the worst residues of barbarism. Evita is the return of the horde, it is the anthropophagic instinct of the species, it is the illiterate beast that bursts blindly, in the crystal shop of beauty.

(p. 85) (Our translation)

In a similar vein, Venezuelan writer Alberto Jiménez Ure published the novel *Desahuciados* in 1998 (the year Chávez was first elected president), where he envisioned many of the grotesque aesthetics that would eventually come to dominate Venezuelan politics and political communication. Jiménez Ure (1998/2015) called *esperpentos* a sub-class of oppressed characters, "those irremediably unhappy beings that kept asking what was beyond the Universal Shell or Concave Filter of the Light . . ." (p. 101. Our translation). In a very poetic way, he presented the notion of a distorted mediation (i.e., the Concave Filter of the Light) that keeps the *esperpentos* away from a certain truth.

In summary, the politics of excesses produce an effect of saturation and, paradoxically, creates more opacity than transparency even if the bearers of this rhetoric of full disclosure claim the opposite (e.g., Julian Assange or Edward Snowden). As Zaretsky (2017a) stated about Trump's presidency:

> Since then, as each new day brings a new scandal, lie or outrage, it has become increasingly difficult to find our epistemological and ethical bearings: The spectacle swallows us all [. . .] Who among us recalls the many lies told by Trump on the campaign trail? Who can re-experience the shock felt when first seeing or hearing the "Access Hollywood" tape? Who can separate the real Trump from the countless parodies of Trump and the real dangers from the mere idiocies? Who remembers the Russians when our own Customs and Border officials are coming for our visas?
>
> (pr. 9)

Even still, grotesque transparency reinforces the impression of authenticity, which is a valuable trait in populism and polarizing stratagems. Moreover, the aesthetic value of such grotesque representations translates into behaviours of active support for these disruptive performances, or at least into complacent attitudes towards the *esperpentic* public figure. Finally, this hermeneutic exercise has shown the importance of including cultural dimensions in strategic analysis in order to uncover what Alexander (2006) calls the sociocultural "script" of "background representations" (p. 58).

Note

1. I requested permission to NBC to publish a video capture of the infamous video where Donald Trump and Billy Bush exchanged derogatory words about women. NBC denied me the permission. Here is the email I received on April 6, 2018:

    Dear Isaac:
        Thank you for your recent letter requesting the use of the Access Hollywood screen grab to be used in your book on the role of images in public communication.

Unfortunately, we are going to deny your request to use NBCUniversal elements in this programme. This denial will cover all NBCUniversal material including, but not limited to program clips/footage, photos, screen grabs, EPK and/or Behind the Scenes footage and logos.

**Please note that there are no third-party companies authorized to licence footage, photos, or other intellectual property related to programmes owned or where exclusivity is held by NBCU.

This letter is not intended to be a complete statement of the facts relevant to the matter or of the rights or remedies of NBCU, all of which are expressly reserved.

Thank you again for your interest in our programme. We look forward to working with you on another project.

3 Sacralization and Profanation in Public Communication

I write this days after a terrorist murdered 84 people in Nice, France, in the middle of celebrations on July 14, 2016. That day marks the Bastille's capture and commemorates the revolution that ended with the monarch's absolute power under the premises of freedom, equality, and fraternity. Around the same time, some countries were experiencing the fever of Pokémon Go, an interactive, augmented reality game where players hunt virtual "monsters" that appear in landscapes or specific places, using a combination of Google Maps and mobile phone cameras that allow users to access spaces between reality and fiction. Both of these examples, which on the surface seemingly respond to radically different rationales, express the central problem explored in this book. The visually grotesque has become omnipresent in the world thanks to our ability to produce, reproduce, manipulate, and disseminate shocking and disruptive images.

In the two previously mentioned cases, the grotesque manifests itself in a variety of forms. In the first example, as with most terrorist attacks, the grotesque moves the public through images of unarmed bodies lying on the ground in *La Promenade des anglais* after being hit by a truck driven by a terrorist. In the second example, the grotesque becomes evident when Pokémon appears in the Holocaust Museum in Washington, D.C., combining images of genocide with the fantastic characters and converging the real and the fictional/virtual (the Holocaust Museum, in fact, banned the game on its premises[1]).

The diffusion of the visually grotesque is the result of a strategic calculation. The terrorist hopes the massacre will have a significant impact due to the massive dissemination achieved by his criminal act. Its agenda of social polarization, intimidation, and fear may potentially advance and modify attitudes and behaviours, and reinforce others. The creators of Pokémon Go, based on different premises and objectives, hope the game will reproduce widely as a contagious virus in the digital sphere. Although they do not prescribe to the visually grotesque, as the terrorist does, they open the doors to create grotesque situations when these seemingly benign virtual monsters invade spaces considered sacred or alien to the logic of entertainment.

Both phenomena are also nourished by the claim of transparency as a condition and possibility of the digital sphere. With the terrorist attack, the public gains the impression—as it has on so many other occasions—of having been in the midst of the horror, thanks to the many videos and photos of circulating through the media and on social networks. The violence of these images—their affective force, as we will later see—derives from their realism, or the total transparency experienced by the audience. The Pokémon Go players, for their part, dive into a "reality" in which the images they receive from their phone cameras (i.e., places geolocalized by Google Maps) are mixed with the "unreality" of the monsters that they hunt. Fans of the virtual game are immersed in a hyper-transparent environment where levels of realism and fiction overlap: physical reality, reality mediated by a device, and reality modified by playful interaction.

In both cases, though the original intent behind these "spectacles" was very different, there is an effect of desecration or profanation. The terrorist, inspired by a fundamentalist religious worldview, desecrates human values—such as the right to life—in the name of a sacred ideal. The Pokémon Go player does not care about the potential profanation effect of mixing the virtual and the real through this augmented reality (as with the Holocaust Museum), pointing to a banalization of the sacred. The religious, in its duality condition of sacralization and profanation, is more than ever present in the public sphere through the transparent display of terrorism or the ludic carelessness of digital games.

The Return of the Repressed

The strategy of grotesque transparency is taking place in a context marked by the return of religion and the religious to the public sphere in Western societies, through the invocation of religious values and traditions by political actors (e.g., the evangelical right in the United States) or debates around religious accommodation and interfaith coexistence in multicultural societies (Bouchard & Taylor, 2008). In both cases, the "revenge of God" (*la revanche de Dieu*) in the words of French author Kepel (1991), has shaken the illusion of secularism in Western democracies pretending to limit religion to the private sphere (Linden, 2014). I will argue in this chapter that the public is confronted, indirectly or directly, with images of the sacred and the profane (the religious in its bipolar dimension) through the strategic diffusion, re-diffusion, and use of the transparently grotesque. I will also explore how these grotesques and *esperpentic* images conveyed by militant groups are consumed by a public that sometimes prefers the bliss of what

Roy (2008) has called the "saint ignorance" (*la sainte ignorance*), where shared emotions (i.e., the affective) overtake discursive knowledge that is often depicted as "secular vanity" (*vanité séculière*) (p. 253).

Etymology shows us a path for understanding the meaning of the sacred, a concept closely linked with the holy. In both Greek (*hagios*) and Latin (*sanctus*), the word "holy" means the special status of a particular place, person, or act after being declared sacred (i.e., after being consecrated). It is sacred precisely because it differs and is excluded from other objects, places, people, or events that do not belong to the dimension of the divine. In Hebrew, the word *kadosh* means both holy and sacred; the supreme and perfect good of the One God is absolutely separated from the world and His "home" at *Kodesh HaKodasihm* (*Sancta Sanctorum*) in the Temple of Jerusalem is emphasized as a space only entered by the High Priest on Yom Kippur. The sacred also designates a psychological and topographical separation that creates a distance to protect itself and that "protects" us from what is considered transcendent and supreme.

Consecration (i.e., becoming sacred) is a performative action through the designation of the holy (Giesen, 2006). Both in its constructive sense (to hallow) and its destructive side (to desecrate), the discourse on the sacred is pragmatic; it not only defines or qualifies what is holy but prescribes action on how to deal with the sacred. This prescriptive act indicates the physical and psychological limits that must not be transgressed, also giving a "holy character" to those issuing the statement (i.e., communicating the prescription). The proximity between the sacred and those who sanctify or consecrate is of utmost importance in political or strategic communication, as we will see in further analysis of the previously discussed case studies.

If the sacred is a physical and symbolic space that must be kept separate from what is not considered holy, then what is the profane? Anthropology and linguistics have recognized the bipolarity of the relationship between the sacred and the profane, or what Freud (1913/2004) called the "emotional ambivalence" of this taboo, given that one exists only because the other is possible. In the topography of the sacred, the profane is always "outside". This, however, does not tell us what is considered "execrable", "obscene" and even "cursed". What provides that sense of degradation to the profane?

There may be two answers. The first one suggests the profane is synonymous with confusion, chaos, and the *tohu va bohu* of Genesis in which everything was a "formless mess", unlike the sacred space that has well-defined boundaries and a well-structured order. The second advances that the profane is the result of a performative act that challenges the qualification and prescription of the sacred, reversing values and proposing actions that degrade the transcendental and sublime. The unholy or profane break morality (i.e., social norms) and thus act to level down objects, people, and ideas through a performance of visual excesses. In a grotesque transparency strategy, is this a profanation or a necessary sacred performance in order to achieve a higher goal? For those who watch videos of hostages being beheaded, are the images virtuous or at least acceptable since they allow them to experience the "truth"? Next, we will explore the complexities of these representations and how they are read through the lenses of the sacred and the profane.

Beyond Horror: Values

It is obvious that ISIS or Al-Qaeda (AQ) propaganda looks to instil fear in what they consider the enemy, either the "near enemy" (e.g., Shia Muslims or apostate regimes in the Middle East) or the "far enemy" (e.g., the U.S., the "Great Satan", or who the French described as "spiteful and filthy") (El-Badawy, Comeford & Welby, 2015, p. 26). Their ideology makes a topographical distinction between the sacred or holy territories of Islam (*Dar-al-Islam*) and the profane or unholy territories named the "Domain of War" (*Dar-al-Harb*). From a strategic communication point of view, this distinction justifies any action or message targeting enemies in the "Domain of War" that will eventually contribute to the expansion of the "Domain of Islam". It would be too simplistic, however, to approach their propaganda strategy as simply the continuation of war by other means, paraphrasing von Clausewitz's aphorism. Both ISIS and AQ have incorporated media, and particularly digital networks, as their sites for political action (Lynch, 2006). They have also understood that the actual and virtual wars they are fighting should rely on decentralized and diffused organizations, even while establishing a central command (e.g., the declared Caliphate of Iraq and Syria by ISIS) or trying (and failing) to maintain an organic unity as a hidden or "dark" organization, as observed with AQ by Bean and Buikema (2015).

These organizations' communications are not only focused on terror. They also function as a way to convey their values and what they consider to be virtuous aims. This is the case for ISIS in particular, which has developed a more sophisticated propaganda apparatus intended to recruit potential combatants (Bole & Kallmyer, 2016) and generate sympathy to their cause (Farwell, 2014). They emphasize certain key messages that resonate with different audiences, not only Muslims living in the Middle East, the Maghreb, or South Asian countries, but also with a young public in Western countries. As pointed out by El-Badawy, Comeford and Welby (2015, p. 5), the dominant themes in the Salafi-jihadist organizations' propaganda are the values of honour and solidarity, the objective of destroying the enemy, the nobility of jihad, and a strong group identity based on the *ummah*, the worldwide Islamic community. Scott Atran (2017), who has extensively studied young militants in Europe, North Africa, and the Middle East, concluded that, "when membership in a tight community combines with a commitment to transcendent values, the willingness to make costly sacrifices will rise. The idea is to encourage devoted action for the sake of absolute values that fuse community and purpose" (paragraph 25).

In strategic communication terms, ISIS and AQ seek to increase their "social capital" (Heath & Waymer, 2014). As per Baines and O'Shaughnessy (2014), referring to AQ's propaganda strategy, these are not "mere self-referential expression of hatred" but a way to increase support: "The idea of increasing the *Umma* (sic)—the worldwide nation of Muslims—is central to AQ theology" (p. 182). How do grotesque images of hostages being beheaded contribute to gaining sympathizers or convincing young people to join ISIS or AQ? What is the psycho-sociological mechanism that explains how, despite the horror or because of it, someone decides to join a radical organization? To answer these questions, we need to explore both the inside and outside of the aquarium, following our interpretative metaphor of the transparently grotesque.

Terror Performance and Reception

Many authors have taken note of ISIS's sophisticated production and diffusion apparatus. Stern and Berger (2015) observed that ISIS engages a network of users—called the *mijtahidun* (industrious)—to boost the organization's reach and exposure online (p. 155). Friis (2015) argued that besides the brutality of the act portrayed, "what has made beheading videos of particular concern in their embodiment of a manifest transformation of an image into a 'weapon' for agents engaged in warfare" (p. 729). Giroux (2006) pointed to the spectacular nature of these actions as redefining space for a "new kind of cultural politics" (p. 20), an idea that resonates with the controversial comment by composer Karlheinz Stockhausen that the events of 9/11 were "the greatest work of art imaginable for the whole cosmos" (as quoted by Castle, 2011, paragraph 4). Even if Stockhausen later apologized for his absurd remarks—explaining that he was referring to "Lucifer's greatest work of art" (as quoted by Castle, 2011, S4)—he revealed something about the spectacular nature of global propaganda. Stockhausen was conveying, to a certain degree, the same idea as Alexander (2006), who noted that 9/11 and other terrorist attacks correspond to a "particular kind of political performance (that) [. . .] aims not only to kill but in and through killing aims also to gesture a dramatic way" (p. 61).

The force of these communicative acts derives from their horrific concreteness, or their *luciferian* character according to Stockhausen (see Figure 3.1). This connect them with the more "tactile categories" (Giroux,

THE BURNING OF THE MURTADD PILOT

This week, the Islamic State released a video depicting the execution of the Jordanian crusader pilot, Mu'ādh Sāfi Yūsuf al-Kasāsibah. As displayed in the video, the Islamic State had resolved to burn him alive as retribution for his crimes against Islam and the Muslims, including his active involvement in crusader airstrikes against Muslim lands.

When the news of the video broke out, the tāghūt of Jordan who at the time was in Washington to meet with his masters at the White House – as is the habit of the crusader puppets – cut short his trip, returned home early, and promptly ordered the execution of the mujāhidah, Sājidah ar-Rīshāwī and the mujāhid, Ziyād al-Karbūlī, both of whom had been imprisoned for nearly a decade by the murtaddīn of Jordan. The Islamic State had done everything it could to secure the release of both Sājidah and Ziyād, but Allah decreed that they would return to Him as shuhadā', an incomparable honor which they had both desired, eagerly pursued, and supplicated their Lord for. We consider them so, and Allah is their judge.

Figure 3.1 ISIS' Escalating the Grotesque: Burning Alive the Jordanian Pilot Muath Safi Yousef Al-Kasasbeh

Source: Image from Dabiq magazine

2006, p. 19), or bodily categories of death, fear, life, and survival in clear contrast with abstract ideals such truth, reason, or justice. These categories correspond to the *bakhtian* notion of the realistically grotesque. This confirms their "authenticity", not only as a truthful performance or representation, but as the confirmation of the "authenticity" of those performing it (e.g., the terrorists as representatives of a supposedly authentic and original Islam) (Giroux, 2006, p. 33).

How do those outside the aquarium decode these truthful, horrific performances? The answer is not unequivocal. The performances have multiple and even contradictory consequences. First, there is no unified global jihad (Tawil-Souri, 2012); there are multiple views on how to understand and justify the actions of different groups, particularly in relation to "near" and "far" enemies. Second, these acts have geopolitical consequences. For example, they have contributed to reframing the conflicts in Iraq and Syria from a "humanitarian" and "sectarian" crisis to a "national security" issue requiring military and counterterrorism efforts (Friis, 2015, p. 737). Third, ISIS frequently personalizes its beheading videos to provoke an "affective connection" with its audience. For example, this was done with the video of a soldier named Berg, where one of the hooded captors directly addressed the "mothers and wives of American soldiers" (as quoted by Heuston, 2005, p. 65).

There is also a more intimate experience among those viewers who enjoy or ideologically justify these videos. From the point of view of the so-called "pornography of violence", this enjoyment (the aesthetic value, according to Tarde (1902/2006)) comes from an "amoral gaze which perverts the empathetic and ethical space constitutive of death imagery" (Tait, 2008, p. 103). It is an enjoyment derived from a psychopathological mindset and an emotional agitation produced by the grotesque images' "reality effect". The ideological viewing experience, on the contrary, is nourished by a highly moralistic gaze about the authenticity of ISIS's rhetoric and action, and a sense of justice that legitimizes the enemy's disgrace (El-Badawy, Comeford & Welby, 2015) (see box *The burning of the apostate*). The ideological viewer participates in a dialectic of horror comparing televised scenes of "shock and awe" bombing in Baghdad by U.S. forces, Palestinian victims in Gaza, and the humiliation of Muslim prisoners in the Guantanamo or Abu Ghraib prisons, with what he or she considers acts of justice performed by the brave combatants of ISIS or AQ.

The Burning of the Apostate

From ISIS' official magazine Dabiq (ISIS, 2015/1436, pp. 5–7):

This week, the Islamic State released a video depicting the execution of the Jordanian crusader pilot, Mu'ādh Sāfī Yūsuf al-Kasāsibah. As displayed in the video, the Islamic State had resolved to burn him alive as retribution for his crimes against Islam and the Muslims, including his active involvement in crusader airstrikes against Muslim lands.

When the news of the video broke out, the *tāghūt* of Jordan who at the time was in Washington to meet with his masters at the White House—as is the habit of the crusader puppets—cut short his trip, returned home early, and promptly ordered the execution of the *mujāhidah*, Sājidah ar-Rīshāwī and the *mujāhid*, Ziyād alKarbūlī, both of whom had been imprisoned for nearly a decade by the *murtaddīn* of Jordan. The Islamic State had done everything it could to secure the release of both Sājidah and Ziyād, but Allah decreed that they would return to Him as *shuhadā'*, an incomparable honor which they had both desired, eagerly pursued, and supplicated their Lord for. We consider them so, and Allah is their judge [. . .]

In burning the crusader pilot alive and burying him under a pile of debris, the Islamic State carried out a just form of retaliation for his involvement in the crusader bombing campaign which continues to result in the killing of countless Muslims who, as a result of these airstrikes, are burned alive and buried under mountains of debris. This is not to even mention those Muslims—men, women, and children—who survive the airstrikes and are left injured and disabled, and in many cases suffering from severe burns that cause them pain and anguish every minute of every day.

{AND IF YOU PUNISH [AN ENEMY], PUNISH WITH AN EQUIVALENT OF THAT WITH WHICH YOU WERE HARMED} [An-Nahl: 126].

This *āyāh* sufficiently demonstrates the *shar'ī* validity of burning someone alive in a case of *qisās* (retribution). The confusion perpetuated by the *hizbiyyīn*, the palace "scholars", and the ignorant defeatists, is with regards to the authentic statement of Allah's Messenger

(*sallallāhu 'alayhi wa sallam*), "None should punish with fire except Allah" [Sahīh al-Bukhārī] [. . .]

> Furthermore, the scholars highlighted the fact that the *Sahābah* (*radiyallāhu "anhum*) punished people with fire in a number of incidents that took place throughout the course of the history of the rightly guided *Khulafā"*

Viewing such horrific videos is not an individual experience. The virtual digital ecosystem offers to these viewers, mostly those looking for confirmation of their ideological inclinations or affective needs, a space where "cheap speech" contributes to social polarization that can be translated into radicalization and violence (Hasen, 2017). In addition, there is evidence that online media tends to amplify the expression of moral outrage and its social consequences (Crockett, 2017). In Canetti's (1960/1978) terms, to enter the virtual closed crowd of believers allows the viewer to overcome their isolationism, confirm and reinforce their value system, and eventually lead them to join a terrorist organization. The decoding of these images takes place in a context of emerging and decaying mediation instances.

Mediations of the Grotesque

Communication scholarship shows that mediation is as important as media. In the global public space, instances of mediation have multiplied. They now transcend traditional groups of reference (i.e., family, friends, or nation) and include transnational relations, networks, organizations, and ideologies (Martín-Barbero, 1993). The global cultural order, or "disorder", is not exclusively emancipatory or disciplinary but—as Appadurai (1996) defined it—a disjunctive, overlapped, and complex juxtaposition of various "landscapes" (ethnic, media, financial, technological, and ideological) that shape and are shaped by the imaginary. The various "non-traditional" mediation instances and mediators fill the gaps left by traditional institutions facing a credibility crisis and disaffection with liberal-democratic values and practices (Foa & Mounk, 2017). They do so, as in the case of ISIS or the alt-right in the U.S. and various European countries, in a context where disfranchised individuals and communities are looking for "personal significance" (Kruglanski & Orehek, 2011) and where the emergence of a "tightening" political culture is more inclined to endorse intolerant behaviours (Gelfand et al., 2011). Viewing the grotesque images of a beheading or burning hostages alive, therefore, should be analysed through the lenses of a "neo-orthodoxy" that at the same time questions modernity and the religious establishment (Kepel, 1991).

ISIS, for example, uses grotesque images in defiance of one of the most sacred principles of Sunni Islam, which condemns unbelievers who worship heretic representations of the human body. The Afghani Taliban, meanwhile, applies this Koranic prescription rigorously, forbidding the publication of images, cinema, and television. Other fundamentalist Islamic groups understand the value of an image in a globalized world. The Iranian revolution, under the leadership of Shia ayatollahs, had a significant influence on other Islamist groups, even in Wahhabism-inspired organizations such as ISIS and AQ. Shiism is more "liberal" with the use of visual images as a tool to propagate faith and portray the heroic behaviour of martyrs. The Iranian ayatollahs, under the leadership of Khomeini, also vindicated the martyrdom of suicide bombers fighting the enemies of Islam, either "near enemies" as in the Iran-Iraq war or "far enemies" as with the Shia militant organization Hezbollah and the 1983 bombing of the Marines' barracks in Beirut (Morley, 2006). In 2004, Sunni Muslim extremists recycled a 26-minute instructional video originally produced by Hezbollah that detailed the step-by-step fabrication of explosive-filled vests for suicide bombers (Kohlmann, 2006). The Palestinian Sunni organization Hamas, closely linked with the Egyptian Muslim Brotherhood, has collaborated with Shia Hezbollah and received funding from Iran (Gleis & Berti, 2012), showing the ideological and strategic cross-pollination between the two main branches of Islam when it comes to terrorism and propaganda.

The 1979 Iranian revolution marked a turning point in the re-politicization of Islam. In his chronicles about Iran, Michel Foucault (1978) observed with enthusiasm the "spiritual politics" driving the movement led by Ayatollah Khomeini. For him, the Islamic revolution represented a rupture with Western values and the liberal/Marxist prescriptions for modernization, through the mobilization of an entire society with a "political will" and utopian ideals. Even if Foucault's "folly" with the Iranian revolution has been widely criticized (McCall & College, 2013; Warraq, 2009), his analysis offers relevant insight into the mediating impact of the Shia-inspired social movement in the Islamic world and beyond:

> But perhaps its historic importance will not hinge on its conformity to a recognized "revolutionary" model. Rather, it will owe its importance to the potential that it will have to overturn the existing political situation in the Middle East and thus the global strategic equilibrium. Its singularity, which has constituted up until this point its force, consequently threatens to create its power of expansion. Indeed, it is correct to say that, as an "Islamic" movement, it can set the entire region afire, overturn the most unstable regimes, and disturb the most solid.

Islam—which is not simply a religion, but an entire way of life, an adherence to a history and a civilization—has a good chance to become a gigantic powder keg, at the level of hundreds of millions of men.

(As quoted by Afary & Anderson, 2004, pr. 16)

The Iranian revolution also influenced the strategic legitimization of violence as means to achieve political and religious objectives. Rooted in the Shia glorification of martyrdom—historically linked to the assassination of Imam Hussein, grandchild of the Prophet, in the year 680 by Sunnis in the city of Karbala—the justification for violence against oneself in order to destroy unfaithful enemies has been widely adopted by Sunni-inspired extremist organizations (Kepel, 2003). The jihad (the holy war) waged against the Soviet Union by *mujahidin* (fighters) from different Arab and Muslim countries in Afghanistan also proved the strategic value of violence against an occupying power. Ideologically and operationally, the Afghan example became the model for thousands of militants who returned as victorious heroes to their countries of origin (i.e., Algeria, Kashmir, Bosnia, Iraq, Pakistan, Chechenia) and did not rely on a traditional central authority (the *ulema*) to sanction the use of violence against near or far enemies.

Another mediation effect of both the Iranian revolution and the anti-Soviet war in Afghanistan was the realization about the importance of what Mowlana (1979) called a "total communication system" that combines traditional communication networks such as mosques or religious schools (*madrasas*) with modern communication means (p. 111). In the case of Iran, Islamist revolutionaries were able to overcome communicational barriers imposed by the Shah's dictatorial regime to prevent access to mass media by using traditional channels such as the bazaar (not only as a place for commerce, but as a public agora) with "small media" (e.g., cassette tapes, Xerox copies, tape recorders, and telephones) (Mowlana, 1979, p. 111). The *mujahidin* fighting the Soviets exploited their televised prowess (i.e., bombing tanks or planes) with the help of U.S. and European broadcast networks and the propaganda apparatus of the U.S. government presided over by conservative Republican Ronald Reagan.

In this case, the multiplication of mediation instances opened the door to the globalization of jihad and broke the borders between tradition and modernity (see box *The murderers and their world*). According to Roy (2008), globalization "blew the link that connected the religious markers and the cultural markers" (p. 263, Our translation). This resulted in some religious rites or norms losing their original socio-cultural significance, creating "cultural oxymoron[s]" (Leon, 1998, p. 173) such as McDonald's serving *hallal* food or the use and abuse of grotesque representations of the sacrificed human body through technological means. In the global market of religion and ideologies, or Appadurai's (1996) *ideospaces*, a competitive logic has prompted the emergence of "strategic syncretism" (Jaffrelot, 1992, p. 595) that allows for reinterpretation of identities and the eventual exportation of meaning to respond to the expectations and needs of those living in different political and social contexts.

Within this context, where radical views defy the normative and institutional frames of organized religion, the Internet has become the deterritorialized space (Mayer, 2008) to proselytize, "educate", perform spiritual practices, and wage vicious sectarian wars (Palmer, 2014). This non-territorial virtual space helps project imaginary spaces (Roy, 2008) to a global community of believers (the *ummah*, according to Islam) who are reachable and can act as a coherent and coordinated collective entity (or the crowd described by Canetti (1960/1978).

In an era of virtual, non-territorial sectarianism, however, we have seen actual movement by followers towards a specific territory, as in the case of young Westerners who convert to Islam and travel to Syria and Iraq to join ISIS. This shift from the "virtual" to the "real", and the closely entwined relationship between them, confirms this book's argument that this type of strategy begins and ends with the body. The persuasion process that leads to conversion happens both at the cognitive and sensible levels (i.e., "feeling the call from above"). This conversion eventually translates into the physical action of changing or disrupting territory (e.g., the terrorists who drove trucks into crowds in Nice, Barcelona, and New York) and destroying other bodies.

The Murderers and their World

From the book *Who Killed Daniel Pearl?* by Bernard-Henri Lévy (2003) about the kidnapping and killing of the American Jewish journalist in Pakistan (Our translation):

> "And then you have the others who killed him, and particularly, one among them, the brain master of the crime, Omar Sheikh.
> "The fright in front of this character.
> "The horror of his hate of everything human.
> "But also, as for his victim, the will to understand—the will to access certainly not his reasons, but his passion, his cold delirium, his way of living and to react, to want and to prepare his crime.
> "The physic of his bloody passions.

"The chemistry of his assassin vocation

"It's not anymore the devil in the head, but the head of the devil
to try to listen the murderous torment that many others before
Pearl suffered, and others will suffer as he did.

"How the evil works today?

"What happens in the soul of someone who without reason, *de
sang-froid*, choose evil, to execute the absolute crime?

"What is with this beginning of the century where abjection
becomes desire and destiny [. . .] (p. 11)

"And then the world, finally.

"This world that is also ours and where the terrible death of Daniel
Pearl was possible.

"This unknown world without landmarks where I have been
involved for ten years, between forgotten wars, Bosnia engage-
ment and 'Afghan report', to watch the origins—including the
affaire Pearl with all its consequences, all the forces at play
and its unintended consequences—allowed me to discover new
compartments.

"The world of radical Islamism with its codes, its passwords, its
secretive territories, its nightmarish mullahs who instil the
madness in the souls, its small hands, its marshals [. . .] (p. 12)

Counter-Strategy and Anti-/de-radicalization

In their own countries, Western governments have launched campaigns
to counter the recruitment efforts of radical Islamist organizations. These
campaigns sometimes use grotesque transparency—recycling visual material from ISIS and other terrorist groups—to convey the horror caused by
terrorists and denounce their lies, as the French government did with *Stop-
Djihadisme* (Ziv, 2015). Other programs, such as the British government's
Prevent, look to effect "attitudinal and behavioural" change in young, local
Muslims who are potential recruitment targets for terrorist organizations
through covert propaganda tactics (Cobain, 2016). *Prevent* in particular has
created controversy; according to its critics, it has stigmatized and caused
fear among Muslims in the U.K., and breached their rights to freedom of
speech and protection of privacy (Graham, 2017). Other efforts in this area
focus on helping former ISIS militants re-join society, but the efficacy of
these interventions (including the Canada Centre for Community Engage-
ment and Prevention of Violence, which funds several different programs)
is far from proven (Dyer, 2017).

The main criticism of anti- or de-radicalization initiatives is that they tend to simplify a complex issue and may fuel violent narratives or even discrimination against certain communities, particularly Islamophobia. Radicalization among young people and eventual allegiance to ISIS results from multiple factors, "including social and economic inequality, political polarization, globalization, declining levels of trust in institutions, disaffection, belonging and identity crises, and discrimination" (Goni, 2017, n.p.). These campaigns are also perceived as an additional source of polarization in societies already experiencing tensions caused by cultural differences, religious accommodation claims, and terrorist attacks (Bond, 2014). In addition, anti-radicalization programs that aim to prevent home-grown terrorism may, according to some critics, "[create] the potential for systemic human rights abuses" (Open Society Justice Initiative, 2016, p. 16).

Another prescription for achieving anti-/de-radicalization proposes to limit freedom of speech and propaganda in cyberspace, and to put the onus on so-called "Internet intermediaries" such as Facebook, Twitter, Google, and YouTube to tackle online terrorism and strike a balance between the right to express ideas publicly and their own social responsibility:

> These giant companies are at an important crossroads now, where they must decide if they are willing to continue financing and disseminating evil, or rather adopt standards of CSR, assuring that their platforms will no longer serve and promote clear antisocial activities. Freedom of speech does not mean freedom to abuse the Internet to promote violence and terror.
>
> (Cohen-Almagor, 2017, p. 129)

In attempting to implement a counter-strategy against the transparently grotesque communication of terrorist organizations, governments, nongovernmental organizations (NGOs), and corporations are faced with the challenges created by a fragmented public sphere; the conflicting rationales of protecting both human rights and public security; and most of all, the competitive views of different groups and communities looking to advance or protect their "passionate interests" (Latour & Lépinay, 2009). To add to this complexity, the explicit connection between these counter-strategies and the realm of the religious, the spiritual, and the sacred—or in other words, their aim to oppose or present alternative religious narratives—prompts cultural, political, ethical, and legal discussions in an already-crowded polyphonic communication ecosystem.

In any case, the religious foundations of ISIS or AQ's transparently grotesque strategy points to the tension between what should be visible versus what should remain invisible (Rancière, 2007), a tension that can also be seen as a contradiction of the sacred versus the profane (Eliade, 1957/2013). The sacred is a dimension that should remain separate, distant or inaccessible; the profane represents "the sensible", which is accessible to the eyes or even touch (Tessier & Prades, 1991). Is there, according to this duality, a "good grotesque" and a "bad grotesque"? More importantly, do some situations or issues justify public displays of desecrated private or intimate spaces or the profanation of a body? In the next chapter, I will explore these questions in the context of public health and social marketing campaigns that use the grotesque and the *esperpento* to overcome strategic challenges in reaching reluctant or prejudiced audiences.

Note

1. "Playing the game is not appropriate in the museum, which is a memorial to the victims of Nazism", said Andrew Hollinger, the museum's communications director (Peterson, 2016, pr. 4).

4 Public Health, Fragmentation and the Legitimacy of the Grotesque

The relationship between communication, strategy, and health has been approached from two contending traditions. The first is largely rooted in French scholarship, especially the meditations of Michel Foucault (1966). Focusing predominantly on the emergence of modern clinical practice and medical institutions (e.g., hospitals, asylums), it views communication as mainly discourse, or the expression of an institutional strategy of normalization and control. The second, which is largely made up of English-speaking scholars, perceives communication as the expression of multiple voices that manifest at micro (i.e., interpersonal and individual), meso (i.e., organizational), and macro (i.e., social) levels within the context of health-care, disease prevention, and health promotion. Both perspectives have contributed to a better understanding of the role communication plays in influencing societal perceptions and expectations about health issues, while drawing attention to the link between power and language within the context of medicine and healthcare.

Foucault's contribution to the field is premised on the notion that discourse—as a pervasive public communication manifestation—normalizes views and practices associated with health and hygiene through a knowledge that defines the parameters of "normality" and "abnormality". In this regard, he understands discourse as both the expression of certain ideas and a pragmatic endeavour aimed at subjugating the body by institutionally framing it within the structure of a hospital or asylum. To this end, Foucault (1980) situates this discourse in a larger context he calls biopower, or the use of technology's power to control large populations as bodies to be disciplined. This he views as vital to the emergence and functioning of the modern nation state.

A more pluralistic perspective, however, looks at communication as part of the discursive production associated with the intentions, expectations, and perceptions of different actors, in a competitive logic or a more collaborative rationale. Lupton (2003), for example, notes that health-related communication is a polyphonic web of texts, messages, talks, dialogue, or conversation from and among different players in the context of healthcare and medicine. Viewed in this manner, discourse is a topic to be analysed as a way to uncover and/or discover the communicative expressions and prescriptions that circulate in society. This implies a methodological orientation that privileges discourse analysis as a critical mechanism for providing comprehensive accounts of the social, political, and cultural dynamics that shape public understanding of medicine and health. Here, the objective is to transcend the mere decoding of manifest content (for example, the frequency of certain words) by analysing the explicit and implicit meaning conveyed through a variety of textual and verbal manifestations.

I situate the study of grotesque transparency in public health communication between the existing tensions of the "normative prescription" and "multiple voices". Instead of homogeneity and consensus-building, which are understood as "normal" or "typical" (Gee, 1999), I propose that communication about health and illness has a disruptive effect on healthcare institutions and practices. I have defined this process as "discourse fragmentation" (Nahon-Serfaty, 2012), a complex dynamic nourished by competitive and opposite views about disease causes and risk factors, preventive measures, and therapeutic solutions, in a context of globalized media and hyper-information.

This context of increasingly fragmented discourses and conflicting views about health issues represents a major challenge to strategic communication. The multiplication of sources and points of view reveals a deeper social phenomenon affecting public perceptions about illness and health that certainly influences attitudes and behaviours regarding disease prevention, early detection, and the demand for new diagnostic and treatment options. Public and private organizations, for example, are trying to convey their messages in a more competitive communicational ecosystem. From a media perspective, Ben-Porath (2007) has explained that this fragmentation process results from the emergence of a "dialogical format" that has changed the way news is conveyed (p. 415). According to the author, the media's ability to "establish dominant frames . . . is undermined not only by the plenitude of competing news outlets, but also by the presence of competing frames within a news program or, for that matter, within a news story" (p. 415). This fragmentation also reflects what Tewksbury (2005) has called the online "news outlet specialization" that, combined with existing signs of audience specialization, may contribute to the public sphere's growing atomization (p. 345). Overall, this trend of increasingly competitive frames and sources could translate into what Lash (2002) has characterized as the "incredible irrationality of information overloads, misinformation, disinformation and out-of-control information" (p. 2).

Fragmentation has also contributed to the expansion of "polyphonic discourses" in the health sphere, where the traditionally dominant managerial rationality of efficacy and efficiency (Iedema et al., 2004; Iriart et al., 2001) are now more often confronted with the emergence of plural voices representing the patient/user perspective (Kim & Willis, 2007; Vasconcellos-Silva et al., 2007). In some cases, so-called "marginal voices" have been able to gain media and public attention and present a more nuanced point of view about healthcare interventions (Hivon et al., 2010).

Discourse fragmentation is also a symptom of the deeper contradiction between the forces of atomization and those of homogenization in the healthcare sector. The logic of fragmentation responds to market dynamics that look for innovation, substitution, and creation of value, and attempts to increase the demand for healthcare products and services. In this regard, news coverage of prescription drugs contributes to the mystification process for medical technologies (Prosser, 2010); in other cases, it reveals a lack of rigour that favours the industry's point of view (Cassels et al., 2003) or even transforms medical experts into celebrities who participate in talk shows and promote books and websites (Sismondo, 2004). This process is part of what Lakoff (2005) has named the atmosphere of "interested knowledge" that permeates the diffusion of medical science, where "companies design not only medication, but also the conditions that the medications are supposed to target" (p. 158). This phenomenon has been labelled as "disease mongering" (Payne, 1992) and even "condition branding" (Parry, 2003).

The logic of homogenization, which is mostly represented by government and NGOs, focus on low-cost solutions (i.e., generic drugs), pushes to regulate access to products and services in a context of resource scarcity, and proposes more control of the healthcare market and biomedical industries. The dialectics between these two forces create the conditions for a multiplication of competitive discourses struggling to gain legitimacy in the never-ending public debate about equity versus choice in healthcare (Callahan & Wasunna, 2006).

Fragmentation is also the result of repeated actual and perceived crises due either to the emergence of new epidemics (Garrett, 2000), particularly those considered media-amplified risks, such as the Mad Cow scare (Powell & Leiss, 1997), the West Nile virus crisis (Covello et al., 2001), and more recently the H1N1 global pandemic, or the side effects of treatments promoted by the pharmaceutical and medical technology industries (Prosser, 2010). Here, we face a discourse about the paradoxes of medical innovations that eventually lead to highly disruptive effects or the revenge of unintended consequences of technology (Tenner, 1997). As Beck (1995) has pointed out, we live in a "risk society" where risks and crises tend to develop as a consequence of the actions taken by modern institutions meant to protect humans and control those very risks.

Discourse fragmentation can be characterized, then, as the consequence of mediated, cultural, and institutional dynamics that create a perception of what Lash (1999) has called the "unfounded", where the truth is constantly questioned by different actors with competing agendas and interests or at least ambiguous ones. Fragmentation nourishes the uncertainty of "liquid modernity" (Bauman, 2007), in a changing and fluid context where knowledge, roles, and expectations are redefined by the information fluxes circulating through digital networks.

This process of growing fragmentation is the driving force that explains the broad use of the transparently grotesque in public health communication. The main thesis of this chapter is that the strategy of disclosing the realistically grotesque is a means to capture the public's attention, and then fix a meaning to the "health issue" that contributes to overcoming atomization and attention deficits in our media ecosystem. The use and abuse of grotesque transparency, however—justified by public officials and healthcare activists as a necessary disclosure for the "public good" (Das, de Wit, & Stroebe, 2003) (Latour, Snipes & Bliss, S.J. 1996)—leads to a number of critical questions. How effective are these strategies? How far can an organization go when exposing the degradation of the human body for the sake of the common good? I will answer these questions by looking at some emblematic cases of grotesque transparency in public health.

Larger, Bigger Grotesque: Fighting Tobacco

The first case study in grotesque transparency illustrates the Government of Canada's strategy to increase the effectiveness of its Tobacco Control Programme, by displaying graphic images and health warnings on cigarette packages. This initiative was launched in 2000, reviewed in 2004 (Health Canada, 2004), and re-launched in 2011 (Health Canada, 2011) (see Figure 4.1). It demonstrates the evolution of a disclosing strategy where its visual elements transitioned from grotesque realism to *esperpentic* transparency. For example, some of the strategy's original tactics were changed to better respond to the expectations and realities of specific audiences, particularly adults with low literacy levels. In response to these concerns, Health Canada (2004) reviewers noted three important considerations: using new images, given that Canadians were getting accustomed to the pictures displayed on cigarette packaging; making images and messages less abstract and easier to understand; and, including images and messages that encouraged smokers to recognize their own behaviours. In 2011, these recommendations resulted in a new set of images and messages being displayed on the packaging.

Figure 4.1 The Evolution of a Strategy: From Grotesque Realism (Left) to *Esperpentic* Transparency (Right)

Source: Images: Health Canada

As noted, the changes introduced by Health Canada represent a clear movement from grotesque realism to *esperpentic* transparency. The strategy launched by using a close-up image of rotten teeth to illustrate how "cigarettes cause mouth disease" or a detailed photograph of a cancerous lung. Parts of the body and organs were displayed without linking them to the "true faces" behind these grotesque representations. More recently, images of actual former smokers—distorted images of an anti-hero—illustrate the stories of those diagnosed with larynx cancer or a patient dying of lung cancer. The images of the "abstract" organ, which were more distant from the audience, were replaced with strong but humanizing pictures.

The strategic choice of "visual desecration", even for an organization such as Health Canada applying a strategy considered "globally legitimate" by the World Health Organization (Canadian Cancer Society, 2014), presents us with a practical and moral dilemma. In a highly competitive and fragmented communication environment, where saturation and desensitization are making it increasingly difficult to reach certain audiences, escalating the grotesque can lead to paradoxical effects. First, the strategy is seen as highly effective:

> Substantial evidence from a broad range of studies supports the inclusion of graphic pictorial images on tobacco warning labels [. . .] Graphic pictures can significantly enhance the effectiveness of warning labels [. . .] For decades, the tobacco industry has taken advantage of the package as a venue for creating positive associations for their product. The use of graphic pictures is an important means of replacing those positive associations with negative associations, which is far more appropriate given the devastating impact of tobacco products on global health.
>
> (Fong et al., 2009, n.p)

Canadian research confirms these results. Depicting degraded organs or featuring testimonials from former smokers who became ill or died appears to be highly effective in reaching the desired audience and achieving an institutional goal. For example, most of the smokers exposed to these images remembered them and said they reinforced the idea that tobacco usage is harmful to their health (Environics Research Group Limited, 2008; 2007).

Nevertheless, questions remain about the long-term effects of these strategies, particularly repetitive exposure to images that normalize what is supposed to be shocking or abnormal (Hastings, Stead & Webb, 2004). In addition, audience members do not always react in the same way to these images and warning messages. Health Canada (2004) has acknowledged that some groups are harder to reach, particularly adults with lower literacy skills, older smokers, and hard-core smokers for whom "the images and written messages are too complex in their own right and, taken together, are too conceptually difficult to be understood" (p. 15).

A cost-effective rationality, however, tends to minimize the potential unintended effects of a transparently grotesque strategy. As optimistically stated in a Canadian Cancer Society report (2014), "the worldwide trend for larger, picture health warnings is growing and unstoppable, with many more countries in the process of developing such requirements" (p. 2) (see box *A visual war*). As we will see in the next case studies, the same strategic rationale for more and greater disclosure of the grotesque is also pervasive in other areas of public health.

A Visual War

The discourse of the Canadian Cancer Society (2014, p. 7) explains the "plain package" visually grotesque strategy as part of a competitive dynamic or visual war against the tobacco industry:

> Pictures can convey a message with far more impact than can a text only message. A picture really does say a thousand words. Pictures are particularly significant for individuals who are illiterate or who have low literacy, an aspect especially important in many countries.
>
> Pictures are also important to immigrants, temporary workers as well as individuals from minority language groups who may not yet be able to read the national language(s).

Where tobacco advertising is not yet banned, tobacco companies use colour pictures in tobacco advertising. Further, the
tobacco industry has often printed colour pictures on packages. If
tobacco companies have used pictures to promote tobacco products, then governments should be able to use pictures to discour-
age tobacco use.

The feasibility of implementing pictorial warnings has been
demonstrated in more than 100 countries/jurisdictions. If these
countries can do it, then all countries can. It is notable that often
in the very same cigarette factory some packages have pictorial warnings and some do not, depending on the country of
destination.

To ensure better visibility and impact, pictorial warnings
should be placed on both the front and back of the package (not
just one of these), and should be placed at the top of the front/
back, not the bottom

Toscani's Touch: Branding Public Health Issues

Oliviero Toscani, a photographer and marketer, has had a massive influence
on the aesthetics of advertising, especially "social cause" advertising. As
the creative director for the United Colors of Benetton, an Italian apparel
brand, Toscani perpetuated and employed the aesthetics of the transparently
grotesque in a number of advertising campaigns. From a strategic perspective, Toscani's aesthetics of provocation contributed to exposing issues such
as discrimination, racism, exploitation, and in particular prejudices against
gay individuals infected with HIV-AIDS (see Figure 4.2).

In November 1990, Tibor Kalman, a graphic designer and Toscani's then-
collaborator, saw a black and white documentary photo in *Life* magazine. It
depicted an Ohio family around the bed of David Kirby, a 32-year-old man
who had been dying of AIDS in the Ohio State University Hospital earlier
that year. Kalman and Toscani approached the Kirby family and the photographer, Therese Frare. Frare's photo was part of a documentary on the lives
of clients and caregivers in a hospice for individuals with AIDS, which won
the 1991 World Press Photo Award.

With the family's consent, Benetton developed a new campaign featuring the image, also contributing generously to an AIDS foundation at the
same time.[1] The image was also used in a press conference to launch the
campaign, which was attended by the Kirby family. The initiative created
a collaborative feeling among those involved in the campaign, while the

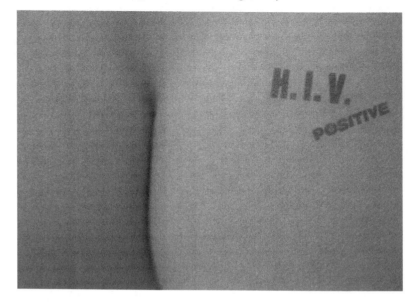

Figure 4.2 Benetton's HIV-AIDS Campaign
Source: Photo and concept: Oliviero Toscani

image of a man dying of AIDS, surrounded by his father, sister and niece, showcased the terrifying sight of a body devastated by disease.

Toscani's strategy went beyond the traditional advertising conceptualization, which typically entails a clear message that is associated with its brand and product's "unique value proposition". His communication strategy transformed advertising into news, with the goal of "reach[ing] people's soul, to invoke discussion of controversial topics, and to bring all societies to the awareness that humans share many similar concerns and that even Benetton, a clothing company, can offer support to worldwide social issues" (Barela, 2003, p. 117).

From the point of view of addressing the 1990s HIV-AIDS epidemic, Benetton's campaign contributed to disclosing the terrible truth about those dying from the disease to a public "who either consciously or unconsciously refuse to accept the reality of such issues" (Barela, 2003, p. 121). In that sense, the Kirby ad was an expression of the "commodification" of HIV-AIDS (Nahón Serfaty, 1999)—as were other cultural manifestations at the time, such as the film *Philadelphia*—that changed the tone and scope of social debate about the disease, and created dialogue and action (Hubbard, 1993). The campaign did so with controversy, while also achieving Benetton's strategic goal of brand recognition and social impact.

For example, the ad was rejected by magazines in Britain, France, and Spain, and some commentators suggested it was in bad taste, as "bad taste continues to escalate in the name of attention getting. And, over time, bad taste can change the norms of culture", according to one marketing scholar (Barela, 2003, p. B3).

The photograph's effect moved from the imaginary traditionally associated with advertising and blurred the line dividing commerce and politics (Giroux, 1993). The image's denunciation character also altered the economy of affects about AIDS, shifting viewers from indifference or hate to sympathy. Nevertheless, the image of Kirby dying surrounded by his family—creating iconic resonances with Michelangelo's *Pietà*—also reinforced certain social representations of HIV-AIDS patients as "helpless victims" (Giroux, 1993, p. 23). The critics, for example, saw Benetton's strategy as a clear illustration of the "commodification" of the body that represents the "gaze of corporate capitalism" (Garoian, 1997, p. 16).

Why could this photograph be considered grotesque? In what way does the image correspond to Bakthin's definition of the materially degraded, in contrast with an abstract idealism? For some authors, the religious iconic connotation of Kirby's dying body—a "Christ-like figure" (Lawrence, 1997, p. 244)—disrupted the canons of the sacred and transformed it into the "art of disgraceful and vulgar marketing" (Back & Quaade, 1993, p. 76). The emphasis on "pathos" (feeling, emotion, passion, or affect) makes this image baroque and grotesque, and has an even more deformative effect "due to the way values are inverted" by the media narrative (Lemos Martins, 2013, p. 139). Others looked at the image's plasticity, which was deformed by the digital manipulation of the original photograph (i.e., from black and white to a coloured image): "At the iconic level, the Benetton advert shows a body that, although still living, looks like a corpse. The body is twisted—distorted, macabre, and unnatural—so as to make one feel its agony in dying" (Scalvini, 2010, p. 221).

Benetton's ad implicitly conveyed a discourse of defying institutional and social conventions. It "profaned" (as we have seen in the case of ISIS in the previous chapter) the "private space of death, dying, and disease made sacred by the medical profession" (Cooter & Stein, 2010, p. 170). The ad also invaded other discursive regimes reserved for political, religious, or medical institutions, causing an "erosion of spaces and redefinition of discursive boundaries, the transfiguration of health/sick bodies in icons modified the discursive regime on HIV/AIDS" (Scalvini, 2010, p. 222).

Fifteen years later, Toscani repeated the same experiment when Italian apparel brand Nolita launched a social marketing campaign during the Milan Fashion Week in 2007 to denounce anorexia in the fashion industry

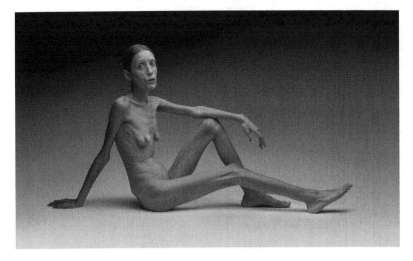

Figure 4.3 Isabelle Caro in Nolita's Billboard Denouncing Anorexia in the Fashion Industry

Source: Photo and concept: Oliviero Toscani

(see Figure 4.3). Billboards portraying French model Isabelle Caro, who weighed 68 pounds at the time, and bearing the slogan "No Anorexia" were placed in various locations. According to Flash & Partners, the corporate owner of the Nolita brand, the image aimed to raise awareness of an illness "caused in most cases by the stereotypes imposed by the world of fashion" (Cartner-Morley, 2007, pr. 5). Following the canon of the transparently grotesque, the campaign's strategic objective was to denounce this reality through the shock value of a supposedly authentic representation of a model's starving body. Caro was portrayed as a walking skeleton that "become(s) monstrous, the embodiment of one's own as well as the onlooker's inevitable death" (Ferreday, 2011, p. 15).

The Nolita billboards captured media attention, achieving significant exposure for both the brand and the condition. Applying the same approach that he already tested with the dramatic photo of a dying HIV-AIDS patient (see box *Justifying the shock*), Toscani disclosed the crude reality of anorexia by showing the model's emaciated body. The image, then, can be analyzed as an expression of grotesque realism: the abstract condition called anorexia became real in Caro's skeletal body. It can also be read as transparent *esperpento*, since the usually beautiful "heroine" or celebrity was presented alongside the deformative consequences of anorexia. Again, as observed in political communication or terrorist propaganda, the logic of "revelation" claims it is necessary to disclose the "real body" to the public, in contrast to staged images produced by high fashion. In that regard, as observed by Ferreday (2011), this kind of campaign is based on the premise that the media's harmful influence on young women's attitudes and behaviours should be corrected through a politics of denunciation, as if anorexia was a "disorder of reading in the widest sense: a semiotic disorder perhaps" (p. 7).

The Nolita campaign confronts us with a duality of purposes. The corporation was looking to improve its brand notoriety, an objective it no doubt achieved. Its other goal was to change attitudes or even behaviours regarding anorexia prevention. It is difficult to establish, however, this kind of attitudinal or behavioural change. Is this image of an emaciated model representative of most cases of anorexia? What seems clear is that through the exposure of a naked Isabelle Caro, the campaign aimed to move from an abstract idea of anorexia to a fixed meaning of the "anorexic body" (Ferreday, 2012, pp. 139–140). But will those suffering from anorexia or who are predisposed to becoming anorexic be influenced by such a grotesque image? In the field of mental health, evidence points to the limited effectiveness of these massive campaigns to prevent such disorders (Cuijpers, 2003). In any case, the Nolita and Benetton ads contributed to a "depravity of aesthetics" that "offers us representations of human suffering, humiliation and death as part of a wider economy of pleasure that is collectively indulged" (Giroux, 2012, p. 264). These images are now part of a visual ecosystem where the public is ready to watch disruptive representations that will awaken them from their attention deficit in the name of health promotion or disease prevention.

Justifying the Shock

Kay Kirby, the mother of David Kirby, who was portrayed agonizing in the HIV-AIDS Benetton ad, said in a press conference: "We don't feel we've been used by Benetton, but rather the reverse: David is speaking much louder now that he's dead, than he did when he was alive" (quoted by Macleod, 2007).

Benetton explained their rationale behind the campaign: "In some countries such as Paraguay this was the very first campaign to talk about AIDS, and in many countries it was the first campaign to go beyond purely preventative measures and touch upon subjects such as solidarity with AIDS patients" (quoted by Macleod, 2007).

Oliviero Toscani, the creative director behind the campaign, explained the "realism" effect of the ad: "I called the picture of David

Kirby and his family "La Pieta" because it is a Pieta which is real. The Michelangelo's Pieta during the Renaissance might be fake, Jesus Christ may never have existed. But we know this death happened. This is the real thing" (quoted by Macleod, 2007).

Toscani said regarding the Nolita billboard: "I've been looking into the problem of anorexia for years. Who's responsible? Communication in general? Television? Fashion? So it's very interesting that in the end a fashion company has understood the importance of the problem, and with full awareness has found the courage to take the risk that this campaign involves" (Bruell, 2007).

Visually Framing the Excesses

The primacy of the image in a grotesque transparency strategy influences public perceptions about health and illness. The pretend authenticity of images of a cancerous lung, the dying HIV-AIDS patient, or the anorexic fashion model is used as a rhetorical trick to capture the audience's attention while conveying the idea that, beyond any cognitive consideration about the causes or consequences of a disease, this is the real, concrete illness. Grotesque transparency contradicts to a certain degree the metaphorical turn studied by Susan Sontag (1977) in her seminal essay, which illuminated the link between public understanding of cancer and tuberculosis and the socio-cultural and socio-political climates of the 19th and 20th centuries. Sontag's (1977) juxtaposition of the romanticized tropes that defined tuberculosis in 19th-century Europe with the militaristic metaphors used in 20th-century North America to describe the fight against cancer showed the discursive mechanisms that were used to fill the gaps science had to explain and to treat these diseases.

The non-metaphorical use of visual images as concrete representations of the "thing" contributes to creating discursive frames—in the *Goffmanian* sense (Goffman, 1956)—that eventually impinge upon meanings and behaviours related to health and illness (Kline, 2006) and shape social conversations about the pathological (Gwyn, 2002). Its powerful ocular impact removes the patient's experience from an illness (Carel, 2008), even as those behind these initiatives claim the opposite by showcasing real individuals with larynx cancer on cigarette packages, Kirby dying of HIV-AIDS, or Caro suffering from anorexia. In any case, it limits the patient's experience to a fixed image, to a moment, or in the words of Rancière (2009): "We see too many nameless bodies, too many bodies incapable of returning the gaze of speech without themselves having a chance to speak" (p. 96).

Paradoxically, grotesque transparency looks to shake up the rigidity of public health or medical institutions (Gilman, 1995), sometimes trespassing ethical limits, by creating a normative discourse to justify its visual excesses in the name of the common good.

The rationality of such legitimacy is twofold. The communicational argument states that disturbing images are necessary to capture the public's attention in a highly competitive and atomized media ecosystem. The policy or corporate argument (depending on the case) says this aggressive strategy is a way to clearly fix an unequivocal meaning about the impact or consequences of the pathological to counter the fragmentation promoted by various and sometimes contradictory interests around these issues. The question remains, however, as to whether there is any limit to showcasing the visibly grotesque to promote the public good, individual well-being, and even a healthier lifestyle.

From Moral Outrage to Stigma Normalization

The brutality of transparently grotesque images—derived from their supposedly univocal meaning—is often a source of moral outrage. The most obvious public reactions against such brutal transparency come from initiatives that push the limits of what is socially or morally acceptable. This is what happened in 2012, when paediatric hospital Children's Healthcare of Atlanta launched a campaign with the slogan *Stop Sugarcoating It, Georgia*, portraying overweight kids on billboards and in television ads to shock families into recognizing the issue of obesity. "It has to be harsh. If it's not, nobody's going to listen", said Linda Matzigkeit, the hospital's vice-president and campaign head, to justify their strategy (Lohr, 2012, n.p.). The campaign was abandoned after months of controversy fed by journalists, experts, and parents who protested against the initiative's stigmatizing effect. A social media counter-campaign with the slogan *I Stand Against Weight Bullying* collected reader-submitted photos on Tumblr featuring alternative "destigmatization" messages such as: "Warning: Shame is Bad for Your Health" (as quoted by Wiley, 2013, p. 124).

Research shows that stigmatization is not necessarily the most effective path for anti-obesity campaigns. According to Puhl, Luedicke & Peterson (2013), stigmatization campaigns were no more likely to instil motivation to improve lifestyle behaviours among participants than campaigns that were more neutral. They were also rated as creating lower self-efficacy and having less-appropriate visual content compared to less stigmatizing campaigns. Nevertheless, stigmatization has been normalized in other areas of public health, particularly anti-smoking campaigns. Following this reasoning, bioethicist Daniel Callahan (2013) has called for an "edgier strategy" to combat the U.S.'s perceived obesity epidemic by pointing to the anti-smoking argument: "The campaign to stigmatize smoking was a great success, turning what had been considered simply a bad habit into reprehensible behaviour" (p. 38). The normalization of stigma against smokers is not harmless, however, especially for those suffering from lung cancer, creating a discourse that blames them either implicitly or explicitly for their disease (MacKenzie, Champman & Holdin, 2011) or perceptions that translate into poor prognoses and a disparity in advocacy efforts (Conlon et al., 2010).

Beyond the ethical considerations, which I will discuss in more detail in the next chapter, the stigmatization strategy poses an identity dilemma, as smartly described by Goffman (1963). The identity of a patient, as a social construct, is the product of tension between a virtual social identity (assigned by others) and an actual social identity (associated with the individual's attributes). Goffman (1963) identified this issue by addressing a similar problem: the stigmatization of people with disabilities. In the field of disease, the virtual social identity corresponds to the normative and cultural constructions of the pathological, whereas the social identity aligns with the patient's experience. The problem with the stigmatization effect of the transparently grotesque remains, among other implications, that social representations of illness and deformity define axiological categories (i.e., health/beauty versus disease/ugliness) and criteria of social desirability. The "authenticity" of these strategies—as in the cases of HIV-AIDS, anti-smoking, or anti-obesity campaigns—tends to hide other factors determining the patients' fate (i.e., social, cultural, economic, policy-related) because of its "excessive transparency". This may follow the "tyranny of light" (Tsoukas, 1997), producing a dazzling effect that focuses the public's attention on certain aspects of a given reality while obscuring others (Strathern, 2000). The ambiguity of the transparently grotesque also defies conventions and formalities, sometimes achieving its critical aim and opening up the social conversation about issues considered taboo or tainted with prejudice.

Note

1. United Colors of Benetton did not give me the authorization to publish the Kirby's ad in the book arguing "personal considerations" about the people appearing in the piece. You can see the original photo and the emblematic ad here: http://theinspirationroom.com/daily/2007/benetton-pieta-in-aids-campaign/

5 Strategy, Transparency, Aesthetics and the Ethics of the Realistically Grotesque

In this chapter, I will revisit the main notions discussed in the case studies and how grotesque transparency has informed and in some ways challenged them. I will start by looking at strategy and its relation to deformative disclosure's disruptive impulse, confirming some of the presuppositions of old propaganda and questioning its own strategic value in an atomized communication ecosystem. Then, I will explore the paradoxical concept of transparency, which is affirmed and negated by revelations made through the grotesque and the opacity of its excessiveness. I will continue with the transparently grotesque's aesthetical dimension, to show that it is a constitutive element of its social value and affective impact and not just an accessory. From there, I will explore the ethics of the invisible as an alternative path to understanding the values conveyed by a strategy that relies on the visually disturbing, defying the sacred, and creating moral shock through exposing the impure, sacred, or the profane. Finally, I will present some brief notes about the grotesque beyond the human body, which will reflect on the relevance of this approach in studying public communication about the environment and the living world in general.

Revisiting Strategy

The study of grotesque transparency demonstrates the ambivalence surrounding communication and strategy as concepts, and towards the conjunction of both terms in the field of so-called strategic communication. This ambivalence has derived, among other things, from the conceptual and practical multidimensionality of strategic communication, which has been described as the tension between the intention of an organization to achieve its objectives (i.e., to plan and control the communication process) and the unintended consequences that every communication process potentially creates (Hallahan et at., 2007). Grotesque transparency, as a strategy, once again puts the focus on audience persuasion through disruption and shock as the primary objective of communication. This means that through the manipulation of a series of psychological, social, and cultural variables, a political, media, terrorist, commercial, or health organization can achieve its goals. The variety and amplitude of the phenomenon of grotesque transparency, as we have observed in the preceding chapters, reintroduces the idea of a powerful source that is capable of capturing an audience's attention, generating an emotional reaction to it, and eventually influencing their attitudes or behaviours (or both). In short, in the era of digital networks and mass self-communication (Castells, 2007), the strategy of grotesque transparency takes us back to a world in which organizations and leaders have regained a persuasive power they previously lost.

The cases we have studied also illustrate how the strategy acquires new meanings or revalues old notions from propaganda and unidirectional models of mass campaigns. The strategy of grotesque transparency is determined by its potential to overcome the media ecosystem's fragmentation. In this sense, the use of the "authentically" shocking or disruptive serves to counteract the atomization of different points of view or even the indifference of a public overwhelmed by the overconsumption of images and messages. Today, it achieves this effect through the public's ability to share these images via the viral reproducibility of the grotesque in social networks.

This expansive feature of the grotesque in digital space makes its strategic reach more complex. In our previous analysis, we saw the range of public interpretations and uses for these images, including ISIS decapitation videos and revelations about inappropriate behaviours by politicians (e.g., Trump and Ford). Although the primary objective may be to cause terror and intimidate the population, or to question the reputation of a public personality, exposure to the grotesque does not always create a univocal result. It can create an almost "pornographic" enjoyment of the realistically grotesque, or incite alternative readings of grotesque images or performances (e.g., a hostage beheading being seen as an act of justice that confirms a values scheme that an individual considers attractive). Female U.S. voters may not have necessarily believed that Trump's words about his grotesque treatment of women were offensive, and may not have changed their vote for him or may have even reinforced their support. It appears the highly affective charge of grotesque transparency opens the door to varied responses or interpretations that not only illustrate a communication strategy's undesired effects, but also the variety of objectives achievable with the same strategic approach.

Given this, we may need to reconsider the critical nature of grotesque realism according to Bakhtin (1984), or the *esperpento* as per Valle-Inclán (1981). These two concepts point to an aesthetic of the decadent, vulgar, or materially degraded that breaks down rigid or idealized schemes, and questions the established order. In this sense, the campaigns by Benetton for HIV-AIDS and Nolita for anorexia contributed to changing the social conversation often conditioned by cultural prejudices or corporate interests. Sometimes, the strategy of grotesque transparency lies precisely in its disruptive potential to cause or facilitate communication at different levels and from different angles on the same subject. This is not always a persuasive one-sidedness but can also be a catalyst for interaction, deliberation, contradictions, and questioning.

The will to shock, impress, or shake means that these organizations or leaders must assume a logic of escalation to counter the desensitization associated with overexposure to this kind of image, discourse, or performance. Strategically, as we saw in cases such as the Canadian anti-smoking policy or ISIS's terrorist propaganda, disruptive transparency must extend to the most grotesque (from decapitation to burning hostages alive) or variations of the grotesque (e.g., the cancerous lung, the patient with cancer) to maintain its impact. This is one of the main limitations of this strategic approach; it must use a competitive dynamic with increasingly more spectacular images or performances that eventually become banal *because* they multiply and circulate in digital networks. It is its Achilles heel, as the transparently grotesque enters a recursive loop in which it runs out of affective value and loses effectiveness.

The strategy of grotesque transparency also expresses a way of understanding an organization's governance or a leader's role. The communicative overexposure of these organizations or personalities is what supposedly makes them transparent and authentic. As in the cases of Hugo Chávez or Donald Trump, the manifestations of grotesque transparency are part of the "media presidency" (Cañizález, 2012) in which communication (in the sense of the source holding a dominant position) becomes the structuring factor of the government (Safar, 2013). It is not simply a form of spectacular politics but rather a constitutive process of organization and political action (Cooren, 2000).

In order to overcome the unilateral vision provided by the strategy of grotesque transparency and gain a better understanding of the social and communicational environment in which it is implemented, a more flexible and dynamic approach must be adopted. The case studies demonstrate that strategic communication must take into account diversity, dissidence, saturation, and even unpredictability to achieve more adaptive and assertive responses from organizations or leaders. The relative success or failure of many of these initiatives (e.g., the Canadian anti-smoking policy or the American campaign against childhood obesity) depends on the expectations, needs, and reactions of various actors. Excessive centralization, hierarchical structures, and more rigid control end up weakening organizations that use grotesque transparency as part of their communicative actions, as in the case of Al-Qaeda (Bean & Buikema, 2015). On the other hand, from the perspective of media impact and public opinion, a more decentralized and less hierarchical structure has allowed ISIS to maintain its disruptive strategy through terrorist actions in the U.S. and Europe, despite military defeats suffered by its central command in the so-called Caliphate of Iraq and Syria (Alami, 2016; Koerner, 2016).

In light of both the potential and the limitations of grotesque transparency, I propose to revisit the very notion of strategy. Although its manipulative capacity still highlights the strategic relevance (Certeau, 2000) of the transparently grotesque, it is no less true that the variability of results is increasingly conditioned by the "tactical" abilities of actors and interest groups. The case studies show the multiplicity of such realistically grotesque manifestations that break with rigid institutional, corporate, or social prescriptions. Thus, I propose to instead adopt the perspective of "strategizing" to understand how the transparently grotesque may sometimes facilitate the emergence of a "organizational direction" (Ate & Thomas, 2016), initiating a social conversation that can take many forms (e.g., HIV-AIDS or anorexia), inciting imitation (e.g., lone-wolf terrorists), or even generating an unanticipated effect (e.g., citizens still supporting Trump or Ford despite or because of crude revelations).

Double-Edge Sword Transparency

The very notion of grotesque transparency represents a contradiction of terms. In the case studies analyzed in this book, claimed transparency (e.g., Chávez revealing the Liberator of the Nation turned into a skeleton, or showing the fragility of model Isabelle Caro's anorexic body) is proportionally associated with excess. Our examination has found that levels of excessive disclosure are closely linked to the impression of perceived transparency. It is precisely in the excess that grotesque transparency is dazzling and, to some extent, opaque. Within the logic of this transparency, however, to show more means to scale excess in a recursive action that moves between the polarity of glaring exhibitionism and concealment.

In all the case studies, transparency is synonymous with what Christensen, Morsing and Tyseem (2011) have called the selective signifiers that function as communicative tricks organizations use to achieve certain public positioning. The authors rightly criticize a notion of transparency that centres on the valorization of an identity or image that presupposes that only one truth should be communicated to the audience or interest group (Christensen, Morsing & Cheney, 2008). Grotesque transparency expresses, in its various political, propaganda, corporate, or public health manifestations, the organization or leader's will on what is the most "authentic" face of an issue, problem, or proposal, denying the possibility of recognizing other aspects of complex and multiform realities.

In this sense, the aquarium metaphor assumes that only the true and authentic would be shown within the water tank. An organization or leader may open the curtains for the public to see what is happening inside, but each unveiling requires staging and the mediation of the concave mirrors, according to Valle-Inclán's (1981) definition of the *esperpento*. This can be more sophisticated, as with the carefully produced videos of ISIS hostages being beheaded or the coloured photo of Kirby dying while surrounded by his family in the Benetton ad. It can also be more spontaneous and crude, like the video of Rob Ford smoking crack or Hugo Chávez's "improvised" confession during the Holy Thursday mass.

Through its excesses and supposedly unequivocal identity or image, grotesque transparency reinforces one dominant premise of our contemporary culture that Brighenti (2007) has called the "epistemology of seeing" (p. 103). By emphasizing the role of the visual image and its relationship with linguistic elements (e.g., Chávez's voiceover narrating the opening of Bolívar's sarcophagus or Trump's off-camera voice talking to Billy Bush), this form of disruptive transparency illustrates the relevance of looking at "the functional logic of visual and/or multimodal framing" (Geise & Baden, 2015, p. 63) to understand the implications of these communication strategies. One of these implications is that, as noticed by Christensen and Cornelissen (2015), transparency is equated with "seeing is knowing", a "metaphor suggesting that having all there is *in view* [emphasis in original] directly and transparently fuels our knowledge and understanding of something (as if visual perception equates to tried and tested forms of knowledge)" (p. 133).

The mechanism of visual framing, like any rhetorical device, has a simplifying and reducing scope. Its cognitive quality—its truth-value, according to Tarde (1902/2006)—derives from its capacity to capture, in a moment, an image, a relatively brief sequence of images and sounds, or knowledge that the public must acquire and assimilate. The pictures of diseased organs on cigarette packaging or the image of a terrorist's victim about to be executed reveal a "knowledge" that leaves no doubt about the malignity of smoking or ISIS's intentions. It also grants authority to those who enunciate or translate that knowledge into images, which can be used to fix the sense of what is seen by the public. This is particularly significant in populist regimes in which the leader has the simplest and sharpest answers about complex issues.

In the case of some radical organizations or charismatic leaders, the strength of this visual statement derives from what Della Rocca (2008) calls—as per Nietzsche—the transparent expression and exercise of the will to power. There is, then, a magnification of the effect of truth or crude knowledge, which occurs in this manifestation of power without complexes or the supposed hypocrisy of those who want to improve a harsh reality or hide behind political correctness.

The visual framing of the transparently grotesque gives access to that knowledge through an emotional key. Within these images or performances, there is an amalgamation between the cognitive and the affective. Horror at the ISIS beheadings, outrage at Trump's words, laughter at Chávez's joke in his confessional "homily", or compassion felt for a dying patient provide a way to understand these topics, beyond the traditional Cartesian distinction between reason and emotion. Neuroscience tells us that emotions are linked to the processes of learning and memory. According to Damasio (2003), "Some feelings optimize learning and recall. Other feelings, extremely painful feelings in particular, perturb learning and protectively suppress recall" (p. 178). This is why grotesque transparency opens up a range of possibilities in terms of the attitudes and behaviours it generates from the public.

The aquarium metaphor tells us that grotesque transparency is a two-way system where the representation that occurs in within the container is influenced by those who observe it and vice versa. The extent to which the source confirms how effective a disruptive image or performance can be reinforces a strategy of provocation. Those observing from outside the aquarium will produce different readings of what they see, hear, or read that may range from repulsion to enjoyment (e.g., comments on online forums about decapitation videos or a female voter who doesn't believe what Trump said is offensive). The question is, what kind of behaviour generates transparency (Lord, 2006)? Or, put another way, what is the public's role in grotesque transparency? A normative perspective suggests there is a symmetrical relationship between the organization and the public (Grunig, Grunig & Dozier, 2006), a relationship made even more symmetric thanks to transparency (Oliver, 2004). A communicative theory of transparency, meanwhile, supposes the existence of a "public that awaits illumination: a nascent polis prepared to receive, interpret, and act upon the information revealed by the state's disclosure" (Fenster, 2015, p. 161). Whether the public's role is relatively passive or more active, the case studies show that grotesque transparency plays a part in how "subjectivities" are formed and translated into "political agency" (Birchall, 2015, p. 195), in the broadest sense of political action as participation in social life. A smoker exposed to the "concrete abnormality" of their habit, thanks to images and messages on cigarette cartons, or a young man who finds confirmation of a values system of "justice" in videos of decapitated hostages, illustrate the range of perceptions and behaviours associated with deformative revelation.

Grotesque Aesthetics

The transparently grotesque has opened the door to reintroduce aesthetics into the study of public communication. It has acknowledged the strategic value of visual or narrative manifestations and examining their political, cultural, social, or even commercial meanings. These aesthetic orientations, which appeal to the ugly, unpleasant, disgusting, or terrifying, are not only mere rhetorical devices used to achieve a goal but symptoms of how organizations, leaders, and people understand and consume religion, politics, health, or brands. Moreover, the aesthetic imbues the identity of a political persona (e.g., Hugo Chávez, Donald Trump, Rob Ford), an organization (e.g., ISIS), a campaign (e.g., the global anti-tobacco plain package/ graphic images strategy), or a brand (e.g., the United Colors of Benetton).

These aesthetic identities also correspond to cultural markers that reveal the "background representations" (Alexander, 2006, p. 58) that shape manifestations of the transparently grotesque. Hugo Chávez's performances, for example, are grotesque in their "highly dissimilar registers" to mestizo Latin American culture (Gruzinski, 2002, p. 125), where he moved from drama to comedy and introduced his distinct, hybrid theology as part of a total *esperpentic* narrative. In the case of ISIS, the focus on imagery in their propaganda is a sign of a neo-orthodoxy that defies the most restrictive prescriptions of Islam about using visual representations of humans, animals, or nature (Pezé, 2002). As per Olivier (2008), this overuse of images reflects a form of neo-fundamentalism that justifies "holy ignorance" (*sainte ignorance*) in the name of a higher objective (i.e., the war against infidels) (p. 252). The revelation about Trump's offensive remarks regarding women during the 2016 presidential campaign aligns with the "society of spectacle" (Debord, 1967/1994), which contributed to the emergence of this political phenomenon (Zaretsky, 2017a). The coding of this kind of disclosure—also in the case of Rob Ford's problematic behaviour—reproduces the aesthetic of gossip that is typical of some TV shows or tabloids.

The realistically grotesque, following Bakhtin's (1984) definition, can be applied in each of the case studies to concrete, excessive, and non-idealized representations of the human body (Kim, 2003–2004). Sometimes, this concreteness is visually rendered (e.g., Bolívar's skeleton, Isabelle Caro's emaciated body, Ford smoking crack) or verbally narrated (e.g., Trump's remarks). Its excessiveness comes from the rawness of the representation (e.g., a cancerous mouth or lung on cigarette packaging), while its non-idealized element is conveyed through "the hero's" fragile or deformed image (e.g., Chávez's confessional speech). The grotesque, therefore, becomes the opposite of any idea of human perfection and harmony (Lemos Martins, 2011, p. 19).

The aesthetic value of the realistically grotesque—or its counter-value—comes from its contrast with the perfect or harmonious. In a context of overexposed and overconsumed visual representations, however, this opposition is no longer valid. In his essay *On Ugliness*, Umberto Eco (2007) notes that some have claimed that "the opposition beautiful/ugly *no longer has any aesthetic value* [emphasis in original]: ugly and beautiful would be two possible options to be experienced neutrally" (p. 431). He contends that:

> In everyday life we are surrounded by horrifying sights [. . .] We all know perfectly well that such things are *ugly* [emphasis in original], not only in the moral but in the physical sense, and we know this because they arouse our disgust, fear and repulsion—independently of the fact that they can also arouse our compassion, indignation, instinct of rebellion and solidarity [. . .] No knowledge of the relativity of aesthetic values can eliminate the fact that in such cases we unhesitatingly recognise ugliness and we cannot transform it into an object of pleasure.
>
> (p. 436)

Nevertheless, why do we still see a relativization of the ostensibly grotesque in some situations? Why would someone consider the diffusion of a video showing a human being's execution to be fair game? How could the aesthetics of a degraded human body become the strategic heart of a global public health program? Before moving forward with a discussion on the ethical dimensions of the realistically grotesque, I will further explore the factor of taste in any aesthetic judgment.

The transparently grotesque's "kitschy" side demonstrates a gradation of tastes and reactions due to its emphasis on emotional effect (Eco, 2007) and its more pressing concern with the attractive over the good. First, the realistically grotesque portrays pathos (or *pathétisme*): the patriotic military ritual during the exhumation of Simón Bolívar's corpse; the colours added to enhance the plasticity—and even the branding effect—of the original black-and-white photo of David Kirby dying of HIV-AIDS; or even Trump's explanation that his remarks about women were just "locker room talk" (NPR, 2016). Next, the disclosure of the *esperpentic* or horrible is often associated with a "higher" knowledge or goal: the science behind the images of decaying organs or ill patients on cigarette packaging; the religious invocation of Chávez appearing in front of the *Nazareno* Christ carrying the cross, or an executioner declaring that he is beheading his victim in the name of the "Merciful God"; and the supposed pursuit of justice through the public exposure of Rob Ford's crack addiction.

The aesthetics of grotesque transparency are part of a totality encompassing the creation, production, diffusion, and reception (or consumption) of what Moles (1982) has called the "sensualized messages" (p. 133) that overflow our communication ecosystem. Since everything is potentially visible—making an aesthetic judgment more "diversified" or "challenging"—we should ask, as Moles did (1982, p. 135): what can we do when we can see everything? If we can see everything, what do we *want* to see? The opulence of these representations, including the grotesque and other forms of disruption, means we must consider the limits of this visual "gourmandise".

The Sacred and the Ethics of the Invisible

A critical approach to grotesque transparency should question the social value (worth) and the values (moral) that this strategy produces and reproduces. The social value of the transparently grotesque, in terms of capturing the public's attention or changing their attitudes or behaviours, is closely linked to the ability to communicate values in a very condensed way. In each of the case studies, the sacred—as an expression of transcendental values or ultimate good—is an ephemeral manifestation that can be quickly replaced by another current event, or a trivial expression that loses its special status in the maelstrom of images that circulate in the digital sphere. In Western countries, where the public experiences the sacred only through the media, manifestations of grotesque transparency represent an opportunity to bring the transcendentally unique "into the recesses of everyday life" (Martín-Barbero, 1997, p. 107). The transparently grotesque, however, conveys the sacred in a way that Bar-Haim (1997) qualified as the "tendency to overrepresent [*sic*] reality" (p. 136). The disclosure of the authentically deformed or disruptive sacred (e.g., the suffering human body or the end of human life) is part of a continuum of "real" events constantly calling for public attention. Paradoxically, the re-sacralization of the secular—even when it happens through the profanation of the sacred as with ISIS's videotaped executions or highly publicized terrorist attacks—becomes a devaluated form of the unique, transcendental, or holy, through its repetition and lack of cultural/communal referents.

In all the case studies examined in this book, the effect of transparency is associated with the exposure of violence in different ways. In this sense, disclosure of the realistically grotesque can play a cathartic or purgatory-type role in what Girard (1972/2010) called the intrinsic unity between the sacred and violence that "allows to organize all the elements of the sacred in an intelligible totality" (p. 386, Our translation). This can sometimes manifest as symbolic violence (e.g., the exhumation of Bolivar's corpse or the image of Christ carrying the cross) or verbal violence (e.g., Trump's degrading comments about women). At other times, these manifestations are very concrete and physical, like the images of a sick body at maximum fragility (e.g., David Kirby or Isabelle Caro) or those of hostages being executed at the hands of terrorists. In its different representations, violence communicates the realistically grotesque's rupture with an order that is in constant tension with the possibility of disorder or loss of balance (corporal, social, political). For those behind the disclosures of such transparent violence, the objective is to re-establish a certain order (i.e., religious, moral, revolutionary, or health orders), with the claim that authentic representations of violence can make the sacred (as transcendental values) intelligible to the public.

To attain this goal, grotesque transparency (in its materialistic brutality) must convey anti-idealism, or the "other side" of the sacred. It does so as an "impure sacred" or as "the *profane* [emphasis in original] as the evil that threatens this sacred form and pollutes whatever it comes into contact with [. . .]" (Lynch, 2012a., p. 56). On some occasions, the transparently grotesque assumes a celebratory, ecstatic tone of the "impure/anti-structural sacred" (Lynch, 2012a., p. 20). This is clear in the re-sacralization of traditional rituals, as with Chávez assuming the role of the suffering preacher who identifies with Christ in the Holy Thursday mass. Other times, the profane materializes as degradation of the sacred (e.g., human life or the human body) or as invasion (desecration) of a space that should be separate and therefore not accessible to the public eye (e.g., the intimate space of a dying person surrounded by his family).

Given that everything must be treated as a form of entertainment to be strategically relevant, the transparently grotesque uses the codes of popular culture to achieve this goal. Susan Sontag (2004) put it brilliantly in her essay about the disturbing photos of Iraqi prisoners taken by American soldiers in Abu Ghraib prison:

> What formerly was segregated as pornography, as the exercise of extreme sadomasochistic longings—as in Pier Paolo Pasolini's last, near-unwatchable film, "Salò" (1975), depicting orgies of torture in the Fascist redoubt in northern Italy at the end of the Mussolini era—is now being normalized, by some, as high-spirited play or venting. To "stack naked men" is like a college fraternity prank, said a caller to Rush Limbaugh and the many millions of Americans who listen to his radio show. Had the caller, one wonders, seen the photographs? No matter. The observation—or is it the fantasy?—was on the mark. What may still be capable of shocking some Americans was Limbaugh's response: "Exactly!" he exclaimed. "Exactly my point. This is no different than what happens at the Skull and Bones initiation, and we're going to ruin people's lives over it, and we're going to hamper our military effort, and then we are going to really hammer them because they had a good time." "They" are the American soldiers, the torturers.

And Limbaugh went on: "You know, these people are being fired at every day. I'm talking about people having a good time, these people. You ever heard of emotional release?"

(4th paragraph, 3rd section)

Limbaugh's rationale is not that divergent from the theological argument used by ISIS to legitimize their propagandistic use of the grotesque. The "emotional release" justification (transposing a fraternity initiation ritual into the stressful context of war) plays the same explanatory role as the "humiliation of the enemy" dictum used by terrorists, which sees the beheading of hostages as payback for the horrors committed against Muslims by Western powers. Suggesting that "these patriots are just having fun" equates to the claim that the "Allah warriors" are just performing God's will. The normalization of these horrible acts—conveyed in the pornographic or "gore porn" code—requires an ethical discourse that pretends to fill the exhibition of visually shocking or disturbing images with specific values.

It would be too simplistic, however, to say that the reproduction and overexposure ad infinitum of the grotesquely sacred or profane—as an over-representation of a violent reality—end up nullifying the public's sensitivity to these representations. The "communicative structure of the sacred" (Lynch, 2012a, p. 136) allows individuals to identify with normative realities defined as "superior good" or recognize the "inferior bad".

First, media outlets are seen as platforms to perform restitution of the sacrality of values (i.e., the protection of children or human rights), as Lynch (2012b) illustrated in his analysis of the controversy surrounding the BBC's 2009 decision not to participate in a humanitarian appeal to help Palestinians in Gaza. This is also evident in the disclosure of Donald Trump's offensive remarks and the denunciation of Rob Ford's problematic behaviour; the objective of those who strategically denounced these behaviours was to restitute an idea of sacrality for public office.

Second, in making the sacred accessible, public communication often juxtaposes it with the profane in a way that defies normative prescriptions (McDanell, 2012). This is what Chávez systematically did by desecrating Bolivar's tomb to consecrate himself as the new *Libertador* and playing the role of the Lord in the Holy Thursday mass, thereby moving the borders separating sacralization from profanation.

Third, the mediated presentation of the sacred implies a sensorial experience (Meyer, 2012), as it has since the dawn of humanity (see previous section in this chapter). In a hyper-mediated world, what is not visible does not exist and therefore cannot cause outrage or shake our moral fibre. To a certain extent, this explains why terrorist propaganda and public health strategies share the same aesthetic rationale to justify their use of grotesque transparency. It is morally acceptable, according to these disparate strategists, for the public to witness the horror of "divine justice" or illness to achieve a higher (sacred) goal.

Even still, attempting to uncover an ethical substratum to the actions of so-called strategists can sometimes be completely illusory. This is exactly what Glucksmann (2002) observed about the destructive "prowess" of Al-Qaeda and other terrorist groups:

> The nihilist [. . .] finds himself as a radical who abandons any measure of modesty, compassion and moderation, the virtues that the Greeks considered to be essential and political. He does not back up before anything, goes to the deepest in revolution ("total"), in war ("absolute"). Proceeds to the ablation of the difference (theological) between the terrestrial and the celestial. Even when he sacralizes the profane or he profanes the sacred, tries the impossible, contravening the equality of mortals before mortality. Thinking that he is beyond death, he plays, has fun, and like an exterminating angel, he becomes his devastating clone.
>
> (p. 259, Our translation)

The same can be applied to the grotesque or *esperpentic* performances of populist politicians (from the right to the left). They may claim their disruptive style of public communication is a way to shake up the foundations of the status quo and achieve some kind of common good; however, the actions of Hugo Chávez and, more recently, Donald Trump's compulsive, confrontational tweeting are signs of decaying presidential institutions in the hands of those who care more about their inflated egos.

Is there anything sacred beyond grotesque images? In other words, if the public does not see the impure sacred or profanation, will it still be able to realize the values at stake in politics, terrorism, or public health? It seems likely the strategists in these fields would answer no: our highly competitive, fragmented, and fast-paced media ecosystem means they must always reduce the sacred, the impure sacred, and the profane into consumable and shocking visuals. By doing so, these strategists present "the total *dissolution* [emphasis in original] of the truth in the fake, or of the sacred in its dogmatic caricatures" to the public (Atlan, 2010, p. 254, Our translation).

First, there is a certain dose of unrealism in these extreme transparent images that moves them from hyper-real to fictionalized representations. For some viewers, this creates a feeling of disbelief in response to such unthinkable horror. Second, the desecration of private space or human life reduces the complexities of the sacred into visuals that sometimes confirm our prejudices (i.e., about Islam), stigmatize the ill (i.e., the ill smoker), or overlap with a commercial brand (i.e., Nolita's anti-anorexia campaign). Viewing the sacred (or its opposite) could diminish—at least in the transparently grotesque—the value of the sacred.

What, then, is the foundation for an ethic of the visible? I propose the answer can be found beyond the image, or in the invisible. To illustrate my argument, I will start with a philosophical anecdote. In *The Spirit of Christianity and Its Fate*, Hegel recounts that when Roman emperor Pompey entered the *Sancta Santorum* of the temple in Jerusalem, where he expected to find the majestic representation of a supreme being, "he was disappointed to discover an empty space" (quoted by Lévy, 2003a, p. 56). Thus far, I have discussed the sacred as a presence, something that is visible to make the public aware of a higher or supreme value. The desecration of private space to instil public compassion for a suffering person; the profanation of a hero's tomb to produce awe and a terrifying admiration of a leader; the disclosure of vulgar and shocking behaviours from public figures to showcase their lack of moral qualifications; or the ritual sacrifice to "repair" the actions of invaders (Girard, 1972/2010).

These examples revolve around the notion of human dignity at a very fundamental level. All of them confront us with the fragility of being human. But can human dignity be reduced to a set of images? Does the sacredness of a value depend on its visual representation? Referring to the Federal Republic of Germany's Constitution, Safranski (1999) says that human dignity is an "intangible", a kind of taboo in a secular world that should be placed beyond the contingencies of "social imagination" as an imperative for moral reason, as per Kant (p. 281). Human dignity should not be respected because it is visible; on the contrary, human dignity is universally sacred because it cannot be contained to any space or representation.

We must therefore return to communication to find an ethic of the invisible. We do so without any prescriptive intention, and as a way to verify what practices in the field contribute to relocating an ideal of good that is at the heart of the debate about grotesque transparency. It is precisely in the capacity to speak about these images, to criticize them and to make sense of them from the "intersubjective relationship" of the social conversation (Pasquali, 2005, p. 88) that the invisible sacred emerges as a supreme value. In some ways, it is about rescuing the *esperpento*'s social critique role (Oliva, 1978) to promote an analytical view of the transparently grotesque that allows us to transcend the initial shock and see beyond the disruption. In that regard, we can identify three main ethical postures: the rejection of what is unacceptable, the transformative conversation, and the iconoclast criticism.

The reaction against the anti-obesity campaign in Georgia that stigmatized overweight children (Wiley, 2013) is an illustration of a broad social reaction to protect the dignity of those considered more fragile. This outrage served a double purpose: to protect them from the consequences of reinforcing social prejudices, and to launch a discussion about the socio-economic factors that contribute to obesity, including poverty and inequality. Grotesque transparency can act as a trigger that activates a transformative conversation about what people refuse to see. Its value (i.e., worth, gain) lies in promoting change beyond what is immediately visible. Although the initial controversy focuses on disruptive images, its transforming capacity is found in its ability to change attitudes and eventually behaviours that transcend a branding campaign with social intent. Finally, we must consider the iconoclastic criticism to confront the transparently grotesque, particularly when it manifests itself from power or terror propaganda. This means recognizing that images are always politically charged and must be read as such in order to criticize them. An ethic of the invisible involves revealing what is behind these images, the interests they represent, and their potential consequences. This is often the task of journalists and commentators, who are fascinated by grotesque images and fall into the trap of reinforcing the strategic objectives of those who produce them (e.g., ISIS or the populist Chávez). The iconoclast is the one who destroys the image to show what it, in its dazzling effect, does not allow us to see.

Beyond the Human Body

Grotesque transparency has been characterized in this book as the disclosure of the realistically degraded, deformed, or decaying human body, in order to achieve a so-called strategic goal. Even if the question of the transparently grotesque in nature or non-human bodies goes beyond the limits of this book, I would like to briefly explore the implications of this approach for analysing public communication in the fields of environmental activism and animal rights. This section is simply an initial attempt to test the validity of this framework and note a few considerations that could be expanded into more detailed research. Regardless, they may be able to shed some light on previous considerations about the aesthetics and ethics of grotesque transparency.

Environmental communication assumes that the way we communicate affects our perceptions of the living world. These perceptions "help shape how we define our relations with and within nature and how we act toward nature" (Milstein, 2009, p. 345). We can extend this assumption to the entire living world, including non-human animals, and suggest that environmental communication places humans at the centre of the world's interactional processes, even though other views have decentralized this human factor from the totality of nature (Rogers, 1998).

The centrality of humans, or our "humanistic bias", seems to represent one of the major obstacles to changing our relationship with nature. Yuval Harari (2016) put it clearly when discussing human unwillingness to "make serious economic, social or political sacrifices to stop the catastrophe" (p. 215):

> Modernity turned the world upside down. It convinced human collectives that equilibrium is far more frightening than chaos, and because avarice fuels growth, it is a force for good. Modernity accordingly inspired people to want more, and dismantled the age-old disciplines that curbed greed.
>
> (p. 218)

Social activism, green advertising, and other forms of public communication have pretended they contribute to reshaping the human environmental mindset, and have tried to do so by changing our sensibilities with respect to nature and other living beings. Greenpeace may be the most notorious and global case of these attempts. Since its founding in 1970 in Vancouver, B.C., this NGO has been inundating the public sphere in attempts "to confront, expose and effect change by creating images disseminated to the media" (Deluca, 2009, p. 265). Greenpeace understands social activism as mainly public communication "conveying complex narratives with engaging, challenging, and iconic images" (Deluca, 2009, p. 265). The organization denounces "environmental abuse that occurs globally" and highlights the existing gap between "rhetoric and practice of governments, corporations and ordinary citizens and to demand explanations for doing it" (Nayan, 2013, p. 114).

Their emphasis on visuals looks to transcend the abstraction and temporal/geographical distance of climate change and devastation inflicted on the planet by humans. At the same time, this visibility is a form of conveying scientific knowledge and "giving meaning" to the science of climate change in the here and now (Doyle, 2007, p. 131). Greenpeace also claims that the "transparency of photography" is a universal medium that can "infiltrate popular culture through media presence by making environmental issues culturally meaningful and symbolically recognisable", through the aesthetics of degraded nature in need of protection (Doyle, 2007, p. 135).

How effective have Greenpeace's spectacular actions and disturbing images been in changing our environmental consciousness? Answering this question goes beyond the scope of this book, but it merits a few considerations. First, Greenpeace and other similar organizations (e.g., World Wildlife Fund, Sierra Club, Rainforest Alliance) have contributed to highlighting the "proximity issue", in bringing public attention to environmental situations that affect our daily lives and for which we are often responsible (Chang, 2012). Second, being more aware does not mean changing actual behaviours. Research points to a disconnect between belief and behaviour, mainly due to the cost of "becoming green" and the prevailing rationale that "the government should protect the environment" (Fowler & Close, 2012, p. 121). This combination of socio-economic factors and cognitive schemas hinders changes in human attitude towards nature. Whether it is anthropocentric discourse (e.g., what is the value of the environment in terms of human benefit?) or "ecocentric" discourse (e.g., where ecology has its own value) (Fowler & Close, 2012), public communication is still far from reducing the perceptual gap between our bodies and the environment as unrelated entities.

Is this different when it comes to our sensitivity towards other animals? One case study that may help to understand is society's general stance on abuse and cruelty against animals. People for the Ethical Treatment of Animals (PETA) believes that animals should not be eaten or worn, and should not to be used in experiments or for entertainment (PETA's mission statement). PETA's public communication has been defined as making "social noise" through shocking advertising (Forrester, 2013, p. 87). The organization's strategy draws attention to and interrupts morally reprehensible practices against animals, aiming to eventually change these practices. PETA achieves this goal by graphically conveying atrocities and animal cruelty, sometimes through undercover investigations that publicly disclose the maltreatment of animals in slaughter houses, pet stores, puppy mills, and animal skin/fur farms (Forrester, 2013, p. 94). Their approach corresponds to the moral shock of grotesque transparency, by confronting the public with the realistic degradation of the animal body.

From the perspective of grotesque transparency, the main difference between environmental communication and communication that focuses on denouncing abuse and cruelty against animals is the visual representation of the object/subject in question. Concepts such as climate change, desertification, or deforestation, even when presented in brutal images of degraded nature, are relatively removed from humans. Our anthropocentrism puts us at a distance from nature, as if our bodies are not a part of it. On the other hand, the image of a tortured and suffering animal is considered closer to us, given its own corporeality and the interpretations we make about its behaviour.

In this vein, the transparently grotesque can help us understand a recent environmental public debate, where video and photos taken by a National Geographic team of a dying polar bear in the Arctic caused significant public uproar (see Figure 5.1). Their diffusion on Instagram and other platforms

Figure 5.1 The Emaciated Polar Bear
Source: National Geographic

generated a wave of sympathy for the starving animal (Stevens, 2017), and the National Geographic team as well as activists suggested a link between global warming and the emaciated bear. Even the Canadian environment and climate change minister tweeted: "THIS is what climate change looks like" (Hopper, 2017). Experts in the field, however, later confirmed the bear's poor condition was likely due to its health rather than climate change (Wente, 2017).

Regardless of the facts, this anecdotal "evidence" fit well within a narrative that connected climate change—cognitively placed in a distant and bodiless nature—and a decaying animal (Cummins, 2017). Strategically, the complexities of science were stripped from the "truth" to expose a crude reality and allow the visible to impose its ethics on the image, fixing the sacred into the contingencies of a media event. The grotesque aspect of nature became "real" for millions in the embodiment of the polar bear, bringing it closer to our own bodies.

The Future Will Be Kitsch

The grotesque has its counterpart in the kitsch, as I previously said. Both communicate emotion from a polarity that moves between the disruption (the horror or the disgust of the grotesque) to the cloying (the cheesy or the extravagance of the kitsch). There is therefore a continuity between the study of the grotesquely transparent and the kitsch in public communication because both depart from strategies that assume that audiences respond to affective stimuli, especially visual ones, which are translated into sentimental states of rejection or attraction. That continuum that goes from the grotesque to the kitsch, and its grotesque-cheesy or cloying-terrifying combinations, has the potential of viral reproducibility in the digital sphere and the ability to convey an emotional state. In this, the visually grotesque and the kitsch share with emoticons and emoji the ability to communicate synthetically emotions, that is, to capture the complexity of the affective in an icon or image.

A study of the kitsch in public communication will favour the analysis of its "sentimentalism" and not necessarily of its "bad taste" (Sturken & Cartwright, 2009, p. 446). As we did with the grotesque, the value of the strategically kitsch will be approached in future research as an

> aesthetic effect in the service of ideological, political, or commercial manipulation. It does so by cheaply tinkering with affects, by presenting pre-digested formulas for interpreting reality, or by offering an illusory appeasement for fundamental human needs
>
> (McBride, 2005, p. 282)

But again, as in the case of the grotesque, the affective efficacy of the kitsch should be understood within the dynamics of production and reproduction, or as Moles (1971, p. 7) said, within the "kitsch attitude" that contributes to understand the relationship that the public entertains with this aesthetic category, its objects, images, and rhetoric. In any case, the problem of taste interests me because it could shed some light on the political opinions, ideological inclinations or even behaviours, particularly those related to issues of public interest or affecting the so-called the "common good" (e.g. public health, the protection of the environment, crime prevention).

The grotesque and the kitsch are part of the same unitary research program that is focused on the aesthetics of strategic communication, and looks to explain the economy of affects that public and private institutions promote to achieve their goals. This program seems particularly relevant in the context where the fineness of big data analysis, artificial intelligence and psychosocial profiling are used to increase the impact of propaganda, marketing, and public relations stratagems in the digital sphere.

6 Conclusion

Change and Atavism in Grotesque Transparency

The study of grotesque transparency leaves us with a series of theoretical and practical lessons. As stated at the beginning of this book, analysing what can be considered extreme or exceptional (and in this case, less and less exceptional) can give us insights into how organizations communicate and the way they are inserted in broader social, political, and cultural processes. Grotesque transparency is a transversal and universal strategic orientation that reveals both changes and atavisms in public communication.

The human body is the measure of the transparently grotesque. It is a body that we see and feel, from which our impressions are formed and eventually translated into actions. It is on the scale of that body that we judge health issues, politics, and wars. From this premise, we can derive the first lesson: any attempt to present a reality that transcends our bodies (such as climate change or the challenges of global geopolitics) will be more successful insofar as it connects with our corporality.

It is precisely this centrality of the body that indicates a dialectic between the strategic and the tactical in grotesque transparency. Organizations—public, private, legitimate or not—use the visual disclosure of the *esperpentic* body (i.e., in its less idealized, decaying condition) to achieve their goals. Tactically, the public does this too, sometimes in the logic of banal or pornographic entertainment, or to challenge the powerful and unveil what has been kept hidden. The recent allegations of sexual abuse in the film and television industries and in politics show the tactical potential of disruptive transparency. So far, they have served to draw attention to this problem and create moral sanctions against abusers. Its effects in the medium- and long-term are yet to be seen.

What seems evident is that the obliteration of the border between public and private spheres makes it more difficult to maintain strategic positions of unilateral control in messages or outcomes. In this context, communication is a process defined by the tactical daily lives of individuals and their technological use. As in the aquarium metaphor, the representation that occurs inside the water tank (i.e., the organization performance) is influenced by the spectators' reactions, in a two-way system that constantly feeds back. This instantaneous quantification of visual communications' reach and the qualification of its reception can prompt a more adaptive tactical or *strategizing* orientation.

Paradoxically, grotesque transparency embodies some of the characteristics of older propaganda: its focus on the affective driver, its ability to synthesize complex issues into an image, and its disruptive nature (sometimes denouncing the established order, other times breaking normative formalities). The novelty lies in the ease with which potentially everyone can be a propagandist. Growing means to capture and disseminate the realistically grotesque through digital networks feeds a competitive dynamic in which organizations and the public struggle to capture attention, achieve recognition, and eventually shape attitudes and behaviours. Excess will continue to be the key to visual communication. It seems that the polarity between the shocking and the cloying (e.g., the millions of images of puppies available online) will continue to mark our economy of the affects. It is difficult to imagine what kind of sensibility will emerge from this oversupply of kitsch and horror; however, our way of consuming, voting, taking care of our bodies, or understanding complex issues will be linked to an aesthetic in which everything—from the sublime to the repulsive—is potentially visible.

From the case studies analyzed in this book, it is clear that transparency is not only a condition that illuminates and clarifies but also confronts us with what we might call dystopian realism.[1] It is worth posing the question of whether so much exposure to fragility, cruelty, and hypocrisy will end up reinforcing the disenchantment felt with institutions in democratic society. The value of "authenticity" is what most populist politicians, terrorists, and some corporations emphasize. In a world in which the virtual is perceived as inauthentic, false (e.g., "fake news"), and subject to manipulation, the illusion of transparency confirms the "truthful" nature of the unsettling. The visually grotesque gives meaning to events in a world of excess, fragmentation, and disenchantment. The language of the ocular reduces ambiguity, privileges the concrete, and facilitates moral judgments. It has become a way of "knowing" based on emotion.

Grotesque transparency conveys a rupture meant either to reestablish a lost order or to question it, hence its moral duplicity. Sometimes, it degrades the sacred so that we become aware of the "supreme good" that is at stake. Other times, it does so with the clear intention of desecration. It is the combination of its shocking aesthetic and affective cognition that expresses its values. Its ethics of the visible are therefore problematic, because what is not in sight disappears from our moral radar, and the ethical gaps that exist in an ecosystem full of images can only be closed by using the logos to communicate what is not visible. Seeing, and from there, talking about what is not seen is the way to overcome the dazzling impressionism of the transparently grotesque.

Finally, we can infer that if the visual, and with it the realistically grotesque, continues to prevail, we will need additional theoretical and practical keys to overcome the rhetorical scheme with which we have analyzed public communication up until now. This study has been an attempt to provide conceptual and methodological bases to study it from an aesthetic reflexivity, in a growing economy of the affects that will be increasingly shaped by ways of knowing and feeling from what we see through the concave mirrors of our screens.

Note

1. The Netflix series *Black Mirror* aptly illustrates the notion of "dystopian realism". Episodes such as *The National Anthem* (season 1), *White Bear* (season 2), and *Nose Dive* (season 3) are, according to creator Charlie Brooker, "about the way we live now—and the way we might be living in 10 minutes' time if we're clumsy. And if there's one thing we know about mankind, it's this: we're usually clumsy" (Brooker, 2011).

References

Acosta-Alzuru, C. (2011). Venezuela's telenovelas: Polarization and political discourse in Cosita Rica. In D. Smilde, & D. Hellinger (Eds.), *Venezuela's Bolivarian democracy: Participation, politics, and culture under Chávez* (pp. 244–293). Durham, NC: Duke University Press.

Acosta-Alzuru, C. (2014). Melodrama, reality and crisis: The government—media relationship in Hugo Chávez's Bolivarian revolution. International Journal of Cultural Studies, 17(3), 209–226. doi:10.1177/1367877913488462

Afary, J., & Anderson, K. B. (2004). Revisiting Foucault and the Iranian revolution. *New Politics*, *X–1*(37). Retrieved from http://newpol.org/content/revisiting-foucault-and-iranian-revolution

Alamenciak, T. (2013, November 1). Mayor Rob Ford's approval rating ticks upward with news of crack video. *Thestar.com*. Retrieved from www.thestar.com/news/city_hall/2013/11/01/mayor_rob_fords_approval_rating_ticks_upward_with_news_of_crack_video.html

Alami, M. (2016, March 25). Is ISIS decentralizing? *Mena Source Newsletter. Atlantic Council*. Retrieved from www.atlanticcouncil.org/blogs/menasource/is-isis-decentralizing

Alexander, J. C. (2014). The fate of the dramatic in modern society: Social theory and the theatrical avant-garde. *Theory, Culture & Society*, *31*(1), 3–24. doi:10.1177/0263276413506019

Alexander, J. C. (2006). From the depths of despair: Performance, counter-performance and "September 11". In J. C. Alexander, B. Giesen, & J. L. Mast (Eds.), *Social performance: Symbolic action, cultural pragmatics, and ritual* (pp. 91–114). New York, NY: Cambridge University Press.

Alexander, J. C. (2004). Cultural pragmatics: Social performance between ritual and strategy. *Sociological Theory*, *22*(4), 527–573. doi:10.1111/j.0735-2751.2004.00233.x

Andacht, F. (2010). Télé-réalité et campagne électorale: le règne de l'index-appeal. *Télévisions*, *1*, 97–114.

Appadurai, A. (1996). *Modernity at large: Cultural dimensions of globalization.* Minneapolis, MN: University of Minnesota Press.

Ascencio, M. (2012). *De que vuelan, vuelan: Imaginarios religiosos venezolanos.* Caracas, Venezuela: Editorial Alfa.

Ate, K., & Thomas, G. F. (2016). Crowdsourcing strategizing: Communication technology affordances and the communicative constitution of organizational strategy. *International Journal of Business Communication*, *53*(2), 148–180. doi:10.1177/2329488415627269

Atlan, H. (2010). *De la fraude: Le mode de l'onaa*. Paris: Éditions du Seuil.

Atran, S. (2017, November 6). Alt-right or jihad? *Aon*. Retrieved from https://aeon.co/essays/radical-islam-and-the-alt-right-are-not-so-different?utm_source=Aeon+Newsletter&utm_campaign=ed6f59f52c-EMAIL_CAMPAIGN_2017_11_06&utm_medium=email&utm_term=0_411a82e59d-ed6f59f52c-69620609

Back, L., & Quaade, V. (1993). Dream utopias, nightmare realities: Imaging race and culture within the world of Benetton advertising. *Third Text*, *7*(22), 65–80. doi:10.1080/09528829308576402

Baines, P. R., & O'Shaughnessy, N. J. (2014). Al-Qaeda messaging evolution and positioning, 1998–2008: Propaganda analysis revisited. *Public Relations Inquiry*, *3*(2), 163–191. doi:10.1177/2046147X14536723

Bakhtin, M. (1984). *Rabelais and his world*. Bloomington, IN: Indiana University Press.

Balle, F. (Sous la direction). (2006). *Lexique d'information communication*. Paris: Dalloz.

Bar-Haim, G. (1997). The dispersed sacred: Anomie and the crisis of ritual. In S. M. Hoover & K. Lundby (Eds.), *Rethinking media, religion, and culture* (pp. 133–145). Thousand Oaks, CA: Sage Publications. doi:10.4135/9781452243559.n8

Barela, M. (2003). United Colors of Benetton? From sweaters to success: An examination of the triumphs and controversies of a multinational clothing company. *Journal of International Marketing*, *11*(4), 113–128. doi:10.1509/jimk.11.4.113.20152

Bauman, Z. (2007). *Liquid times: Living in an age of uncertainty*. Cambridge, UK: Polity Press.

Bean, H., & Buikema, R. J. (2015). Deconstituting al-Qa'ida: CCO theory and the decline and dissolution of hidden organizations. *Management Communication Quarterly*, *29*(4), 512–538. doi:10.1177/0893318915597300

Beck, U. (1995). A reinvençao da politica: rumo a uma teoria da modernizaçao reflexiva. In A. Giddens, U. Beck, & S. Lash (Eds.), *Modernizaçao Reflexiva: Política, Tradiçao e Estética na Ordem Social Moderna* (pp. 11–72). Sao Paulo, Brasil: Editora da UNESP.

Ben-Porath, E. N. (2007). Internal fragmentation of the news: Television news in dialogical format and its consequences for journalism. *Journalism Studies*, *8*, 414–431. doi:10.1080/14616700701276166

Bernays, E. (1928/2005). *Propaganda*. Brooklyn, NY: Ig Publishing.

Birchall, C. (2015). "Data.gov-in-a-box": Delimiting transparency. *European Journal of Social Theory*, *18*(2), 185–202. doi:10.1177/1368431014555259

Bisbal, M. (Ed.). (2009). *Hegemonía y control comunicacional*. Caracas, Venezuela: Editorial Alfa—UCAB.

Bisbal, M. (2013). Un nuevo régimen comunicativo: Política, poder y comunicaciones en tiempos de Chávez. In M. Bisbal (Ed.), *Saldo en rojo: Comunicaciones y cultura en la era bolivariana* (pp. 49–67). Caracas, Venezuela: Ediciones UCAB—Konrad Adenauer Stiftung.

Bole, R., & Kallmyer, K. (2016). Combatting the Islamic state's digital dominance: Revitalizing U.S. Communication strategy. *The Washington Quarterly, 39*(1), 29–48. doi:10.1080/0163660X.2016.1170478

Bond, M. (2014, September 10). Why westerners are driven to join the jihadist fight. *New Scientist*. Retrieved from www.newscientist.com/article/mg22329861-700-why-westerners-are-driven-to-join-the-jihadist-fight/

Borges, J. L. (1955/2011, November–December). L'illusion comique. *Revista Sur, 237*, 9–10. Retrieved from http://borgestodoelanio.blogspot.ca/2015/10/jorge-luis-borges-lillusion-comique.html

Bouchard, G., & Taylor, C. (2008). *Building the future: A time for reconciliation.* Abridged Report. Québec & Canada: Gouvernement du Québec.

Briceño Guerrero, J. M. (1997). *El laberinto de los tres minotauros.* Caracas, Venezuela: Monte Ávila Editores Latinoamericana.

Brighenti, A. (2007). Visibility: A category for the social sciences. *Current Sociology, 55*(3), 323–342. doi:10.1177/0011392107076079

Brooker, C. (2011, December 1). Charlie Brooker: The dark side of our gadget addiction. *The Guardian*. Retrieved from www.theguardian.com/technology/2011/dec/01/charlie-brooker-dark-side-gadget-addiction-black-mirror

Bruell, A. (2007, October 1). Nolita. *PR Week*. Retrieved from www.prweek.com/article/1255740/nolita

Bullock, P. (2016, October 8). Transcript: Donald trump's taped comments about women. *The New York Times*. Retrieved from www.nytimes.com/2016/10/08/us/donald-trump-tape-transcript.html

Callahan, D. (2013). Obesity: Chasing an elusive epidemic. *The Hastings Center Report, 43*(1), 34–40. doi:10.1002/hast.114

Callahan, D., & Wasunna, A. A. (2006). *Medicine and the market: Equity v. choice.* Baltimore, MD: The Johns Hopkins University Press.

Campanella, N. H. (1980). *Valle Inclán: materia y forma del esperpento.* Buenos Aires, Argentina: Epsilon Editora & S.R.L.

Canadian Cancer Society. (2014). *Cigarette package health warnings: International status report* (4th ed.). Canadian Cancer Society & Société Canadienne du Cancer.

Canetti, E. (1960/1978). *Crowds and power.* New York, NY: Continuum.

Cañizález, A. (2012). *Hugo Chávez, la presidencia mediatica.* Caracas, Venezuela: Editorial Alfa.

Capriles, C. (2006). La enciclopedia del chavismo o hacia una teología del populismo. *Revista venezolana de Ciencia Política, 29*, 73–92.

Carel, H. (2008). *Illness.* Stocksfield, UK: Acumen Publishing Limited.

Carrera Damas, G. (2011). *El bolivarianismo-militarismo, una ideología de reemplazo.* Caracas, Venezuela: Editorial Alfa.

Carroll, N. (1990/2004). *The philosophy of horror or paradoxes of the heart.* New York, NY & London, UK: Routledge.

Cartner-Morley, J. (2007, September 26). Shock anorexia billboard annoys fashion designers. *The Guardian*. Retrieved from www.theguardian.com/world/2007/sep/26/advertising.fashion

Cassels, A., Hughes, M. A., Cole, C., Mintzes, B., Lexchin, J., & McCormack, J. P. (2003). Drugs in the news: An analysis of Canadian newspaper coverage of new prescription drugs. *Canadian Medical Association Journal, 168*, 1133–1137.

Castells, M. (2007). Communication, power and counter-power in the network society. *International Journal of Communication, 1*, 238–266.

Castle, T. (2011, August 27). Stockhausen, Karlheinz: The unsettling question of the Sublime (The Encyclopedia of 9/11). *New York Magazine*. Retrieved from http://nymag.com/news/9-11/10th-anniversary/karlheinz-stockhausen/

Certeau (de), M. (2000). *La invención de lo cotidiano: I. Artes de hacer*. México, DF: Universidad Iberoamericana & Biblioteca Francisco Xavier Clavigero.

Chang, C. T. (2012). Are guilt appeals a panacea in green advertising? The right formula of issue proximity and environmental consciousness. *International Journal of Advertising, 31*(4), 741–771. doi:10.2501/IJA-31-4-741-771

Chávez, H. (2012, April 5). *Misa de acción de gracias por la salud del Comandante Presidente Hugo Chávez*. Retrieved from www.todochavez.gob.ve/todochavez/175-misa-de-accion-de-gracias-por-la-salud-del-comandante-presidente-hugo-chavez

Chirinos, M. (2013). Hitos Comunicacionales del Proceso Revolucionario (1999–2012). In M. Bisbal (Ed.), *Saldo en rojo: Comunicaciones y cultura en la era bolivariana* (pp. 133–155). Caracas, Venezuela: Ediciones UCAB—Konrad Adenauer Stiftung.

Christensen, L. T., & Cornelissen, J. (2015). Organizational transparency as myth and metaphor. *European Journal of Social Theory, 18*(2), 132–149. doi:10.1177/1368431014555256

Christensen, L. T., Morsing, M., & Cheney, G. (2008). *Corporate communications: Convention, complexity, and critique*. Thousand Oaks, CA: Sage Publications.

Christensen, L. T., Morsing, M., & Thyssen, O. (2011). The polyphony of corporate social responsibility: Deconstructing accountability and transparency in the context of identity and hypocrisy. In G. Cheney, S. May, & D. Munshi (Eds.), *The handbook of communication ethics* (pp. 457–474). New York, NY: Routledge Curzon.

Citton, Y. (2008). Entre l'économie psychique de Spinoza et l'inter-psychologie économique de Tarde. In Y. Citton & F. Lordon (Eds.) (sous la direction), *Spinoza et les sciences sociales: De la puissance de la multitude à l'économie des affects* (pp. 71–106). Paris: Éditions Amsterdam.

Cobain, I. (2016, October 19). UK's Prevent counter-radicalisation policy "badly flawed". *The Guardian*. Retrieved from www.theguardian.com/uk-news/2016/oct/19/uks-prevent-counter-radicalisation-policy-badly-flawed

Cohen-Almagor, R. (2017). The role of internet intermediaries in tackling terrorism online. *Fordham Law Review, 86*(2), 425–453. Retrieved from https://fordhamlawreview.org/wp-content/uploads/2017/10/Cohen-Almagor_November_v86.pdf

Conlon, A., Gilbert, D., Jones, B., & Aldredge, P. (2010). Stacked stigma: Oncology social workers' perceptions of the lung cancer experience. *Journal of Psychosocial Oncology, 28*(1), 98–115. doi:10.1080/07347330903438982.

Cooper, R. (1993). *Información e institución: Dos ensayos sobre estética y comunicación en el análisis organizacional*. Caracas, Venezuela: Ediciones IESA.

Cooren, F. (2000). *The organizing properties of communication.* Amsterdam, Netherlands: John Benjamins.

Cooter, R., & Stein, C. (2010). Visual imagery and epidemics in the twentieth century. In D. Serlin (Ed.), *Imagining illness: Public health and visual culture* (pp. 169–192). Minneapolis, MN: University of Minnesota Press.

Coronil, F. (1997). *The magical state. Nature, money, and modernity in Venezuela.* Chicago, IL & London, UK: University of Chicago Press.

Covello, V., Peters, R., Wojtecki, J., & Hyde, R. (2001). Risk communication, the West Nile virus epidemic, and bio-terrorism: Responding to the communication challenges posed by the intentional or unintentional release of a pathogen in an urban setting. *Journal of Urban Health: Bulletin of the New York Academy of Medicine, 78,* 382–391. doi:10.1093/jurban/78.2.382

Crockett, M. J. (2017). Moral outrage in the digital age. *Nature Human Behaviour, 1,* 769–771. doi:10.1038/s41562-017-0213-3

Cuijpers, P. (2003). Examining the effects of prevention programs on the incidence of new cases of mental disorders: The lack of statistical power. *American Journal of Psychiatry, 160*(8), 1385–1391. doi:10.1176/appi.ajp.160.8.1385

Cummins, E. (2017, December 11). Is that starving polar bear dying from climate change? Probably not. *Slate.* Retrieved from www.slate.com/articles/health_and_science/science/2017/12/the_viral_photo_of_a_starving_polar_bear_might_be_dying_of_cancer_not_climate.html

Damasio, A. R. (2003). *Looking for Spinoza: Joy, sorrow, and the feeling brain.* Orlando, FL: Harcourt, Inc.

Darias Príncipe, A. (1996). Iconografía bolivariana en el Panteón de Caracas: la necesidad de un mito. *Norba-Arte, XVI,* 277–298.

Das, E. H. H. J., de Wit, J. B. F., & Stroebe, W. (2003). Fear appeals motivate acceptance of action recommendations: Evidence for a positive bias in the processing of persuasive messages. *Personality and Social Psychology Bulletin, 29*(5), 650–664. doi:10.1177/0146167203251527

Debord, G. (1967/1994). *The society of the spectacle.* New York, NY: Zone Books.

Debray, R. (1981). *Critique de la raison politique.* Paris: Gallimard.

Della Rocca, M. (2008). *Spinoza.* New York, NY: Routledge.

Deluca, K. M. (2009). Greenpeace international media analyst reflects on communicating climate change. *Environmental Communication: A Journal of Nature and Culture, 3*(2), 263–269. doi:10.1080/17524030902972734

Domenach, J. M. (1979). *La propagande politique.* Paris: Presses Universitaires de France.

Doyle, J. (2007). Picturing the clima(c)tic: Greenpeace and the representational politics of climate change communication. *Science as Culture, 16*(2), 129–150. doi:10.1080/09505430701368938

Dyer, E. (2017, November 23). Federal government not tracking interventions with returning ISIS fighters. *CBC News.* Retrieved from www.cbc.ca/news/politics/deradicalization-canada-isis-fighters-program-1.4414999

Eco, U. (2007). *On ugliness.* London, UK: Harvill Secker.

Eliade, M. (1957/2013). *Le sacré et le profane.* Paris: Gallimard & Folio Essais.

El-Badawy, E., Comerford, M., & Welby, P. (2015). *Inside the jihadi mind: Understanding ideology and propaganda*. London, UK: Center on Religion 0026 Geopolitics.

Environics Research Group Limited. (2007). *The health effects of tobacco and health warning messages on cigarette packages. Survey of youth*. Final report. Prepared for Health Canada.

Environics Research Group Limited. (2008). *The health effects of tobacco and health warning messages on cigarette packages survey of adults and adult smokers*. Final Report. Prepared for Health Canada.

Farwell, J. P. (2014). The media strategy of ISIS. *Survival, 56*(6), 49–55. doi:10.1080/00396338.2014.985436

Fenster, M. (2015). Transparency in search of a theory. *European Journal of Social Theory, 18*(2), 150–167. doi:10.1177/1368431014555257

Ferreday, D. (2011). Haunted bodies: Visual cultures of anorexia. *Borderlands e-Journal: New Spaces in the Humanities, 10*(2), 7. Retrieved from www.borderlands.net.au/vol10no2_2011/ferreday_bodies.pdf

Ferreday, D. (2012). Anorexia and abjection: A review essay. *Body & Society, 18*(2), 139–155. doi:10.1177/1357034X12440830

Foa, R. S., & Mounk, Y. (2017). The signs of deconsolidation. *Journal of Democracy, 28*(1), 5–16. Retrieved from www.journalofdemocracy.org/article/signs-deconsolidation

Fong, G. T., Hammond, D., & Hitchman, S. C. (2009). The impact of pictures on the effectiveness of tobacco warnings. *Bulletin of the World Health Organization, 87*, 640–643. doi:10.2471/BLT.09.069575

Forrester, M. (2013). PETA making social noise: A perspective on shock advertising. *Portuguese Journal of Social Science, 12*(1), 85–100.

Foucault, M. (1966). *La Naissance de la Clinique*. Paris: Presses Universitaires de France.

Foucault, M. (1968). *L'Archéologie du Savoir*. Paris: Gallimard.

Foucault, M. (1978/2005). *What are the Iranians dreaming about?* University of Chicago Press. Retrieved from www.press.uchicago.edu/Misc/Chicago/007863.html

Foucault, M. (1980). *Power/knowledge: Selected interviews & other writings* (Colin Gordon, Ed.). New York, NY: Pantheon Books.

Fowler, A., & Close, A. (2012). It ain't easy being green: Macro, meso, and micro green advertising agendas. *Journal of Advertising, 41*(4), 119–132. doi:10.1080/00913367.2012.10672461

Freud, S. (1913/2004). *Totem and taboo: Some points of agreement between the mental lives of savages and neurotics*. London, UK: Routledge.

Freud, S. (1930/1955). *El malestar en la cultura*. Buenos Aires, Argentina: Santiago Rueda.

Friis, S. M. (2015). "Beyond anything we have ever seen": Beheading videos and the visibility of violence in the war against ISIS. *International Affairs, 91*(4), 725–746. doi:10.1111/1468-2346.12341

Galloway, A. (2011). Are some things unrepresentable? *Theory, Culture & Society, 28*(7–8), 85–102. doi:10.1177/0263276411423038

Garoian, C. (1997). Art, education and the aesthetics of health in the age of AIDS. *Studies in Art Education, 39*(1), 6–23.

Garrett, L. (2000). *Betrayal of trust: The collapse of global public health*. New York, NY: Hyperion.

Gee, J. P. (1999). *An introduction to discourse analysis: Theory and method*. London, UK & New York, NY: Routledge.

Geise, S., & Baden, C. (2015). Putting the image back into the frame: Modeling the linkage between visual communication and frame-processing theory. *Communication Theory, 25*(1), 46–69. doi:10.1111/comt.12048

Gelfand, M. J., Raver, J. L., Nishii, L., Leslie, L. M., Lun, J., Lim, B. C., . . . Yamaguchi, S. (2011). Differences between tight and loose cultures: A 33-nation study. *Science, 332*(6033), 1100–1104. doi:10.1126/science.1197754

Gherardi, S., & Strati, A. (2017). Luigi pareyson's estetica: Teoria della formatività and its implication for organization studies. *Academy of Management Review, 42*(4), 745–755. doi:10.5465/amr.2016.0165

Giesen, B. (2006). Performing the sacred: A durkheimian perspective on the performative turn in social sciences. In J. C. Alexander, B. Giesen, & J. L. Mast (Eds.), *Social performance. Symbolic action, cultural pragmatics, and ritual* (pp. 325–367). New York, NY: Cambridge University Press.

Gilman, S. L. (1995). *Picturing health and illness: Images of identity and difference*. Baltimore, MD & London, UK: The John Hopkins University Press.

Gilovich, T., Husted Medvec, V., & Savitsky, K. (1998). The illusion of transparency: Biased assessments of others' ability to read one's emotional states. *Journal of Personality and Social Psychology, 75*(2), 332–346. doi:10.1037/0022–3514. 75.2.332

Girard, R. (1972/2010). *La violence et le sacré*. Paris: Fayard & Pluriel.

Giroux, H. (1993). Consuming social change: The "United Colors of Benetton". *Cultural Critique, 26*, 5–32. doi:10.2307/1354454

Giroux, H. (2012). Disturbing pleasures: Murderous images and the aesthetics of depravity. *Third Text, 26*(3), 259–273. doi:10.1080/09528822.2012.679036

Giroux, H. A. (2006). *Beyond the space of terrorism: Rethinking politics in the society of the image. This essay draws on ideas from the author's book, beyond the spectacle of terrorism: Global uncertainty and the challenge of the new media*. Boulder, CO: Paradigm Publishers. Retrieved from https://radicalimagination. institute/wp-content/uploads/2017/02/giroux-2007-1.pdf

Gleis, J. L., & Berti, B. (2012). *Hezbollah and Hamas: A comparative study*. Baltimore, MD: The Johns Hopkins University Press.

Glucksmann, A. (2002). *Dostoievski en Manhattan*. Madrid: Taurus.

Goffman, E. (1956). *The presentation of self in everyday life*. Edinburgh: University of Edinburgh & Social Sciences Research Centre.

Goffman, E. (1963). *Stigma: Notes on the management of spoiled identity*. Englewood Cliffs, NJ: Prentice-Hall, Inc.

Goni, C. (2017, October 27). The truth about terror and youth radicalization. *Open Society Foundations*. Retrieved from www.opensocietyfoundations.org/voices/ truth-about-terror-and-youth-radicalization

Graham, C. (2017, May 26). What is the anti-terror prevent programme and why is it controversial? *The Telegraph*. Retrieved February 25, 2018, from www.telegraph.co.uk/news/0/anti-terror-prevent-programme-controversial/

Green, J. E. (2010). *The eyes of the people: Democracy in an age of spectatorship*. New York, NY: Oxford University Press.

Grunig, J. E. (2009). Paradigms of global public relations in an age of digitalisation. *PRism*, *6*(2). Retrieved from http://shonaliburke.com/wp-content/uploads/2010/10/GRUNIG.pdf

Grunig, J. E., Grunig, L. A., & Dozier, D. M. (2006). The excellence theory. In C. H. Botan & V. Hazleton (Eds.), *Public relations theory II* (pp. 21–62). Mahway, NJ: Lawrence Erlbaum Associates, Publishers.

Gruzinski, S. (2002). *The mestizo mind: The intellectual dynamics of colonization and globalization*. New York, NY & London, UK: Routledge.

Gupta, A., & Mason, M. (Eds.). (2014). *Transparency in global environmental governance: Critical perspectives*. Cambridge, MA: MIT Press.

Gutiérrez, G. (1971). *Teología de la liberación*. Lima, Perú: CEP, Perspectivas.

Gwyn, R. (2002). *Communicating health and illness*. London: Sage Publications.

Habermas, J. (1993). Actions, actes de parole, interactions médiatisées par le langage et monde vécu. In J. Habermas (Ed.), *La pensée postmétaphysique: essaies philosophiques* (pp. 65–83). Paris: Armand Collin.

Hallahan, K., Holtzhausen, D., van Ruler, B., Verčič, D., & Sriramesh, K. (2007). Defining strategic communication. *International Journal of Strategic Communication*, *1*(1), 3–35. doi:10.1080/15531180701285244

Harari, Y. N. (2016). *Homo deus: A brief history of tomorrow*. Toronto & Canada: Signal.

Hardt, M., & Negri, A. (2004). *Multitude: War and democracy in the age of empire*. New York, NY: The Penguin Press.

Hasen, R. L. (2017, August 11). Cheap speech and what it has done (to American Democracy). *First Amendment Law Review*. Retrieved from https://ssrn.com/abstract=3017598

Hastings, G., Stead, M., & Webb, J. (2004). Fear appeals in social marketing: Strategic and ethical reasons for concern. *Psychology & Marketing*, *21*(11), 961–986. doi:10.1002/mar.20043

Health Canada. (2004). *Building on success. A proposal for new health related information on tobacco product labels*. A Consultation Paper. Health Canada. Tobacco Control Programme.

Health Canada. (2011, January 20). Minister Aglukkaq marks national non-smoking week with a focus on smoking prevention for youth. *Health Canada News Release*. Retrieved from www.hc-sc.gc.ca/ahc-asc/media/nr-cp/_2011/2011_08-eng.php

Heath, R. L., & Waymer, D. (2014). Terrorism: Social capital, social construction, and constructive society? *Public Relations Inquiry*, *3*(2), 227–244.

Heuston, S. (2005). Weapons of mass instruction: Terrorism, propaganda film, politics, and us: New media, new meanings. *Studies in Popular Culture*, *27*(3), 59–73. Retrieved from www.jstor.org/stable/23414997

Hivon, M., Lehoux, P., Denis, J. L., & Rock, M. (2010). Marginal voices in the media coverage of controversial health interventions: How do they contribute to the public understanding of science? *Public Understanding of Science, 19*, 34–51. doi:10.1177/0963662508088668

Hobsbawm, E., & Ranger, T. (1983). *The Invention of Tradition.* Cambridge: Cambridge University Press.

Hong, S. (2016). What gender gap? *The New Republic.* Retrieved from https://newrepublic.com/minutes/138601/gender-gap-exit-polls-show-white-women-voters-actually-preferred-trump-clinton)

Hopper, T. (2017, December 12). What everybody got wrong about that viral video of a starving polar bear. *National Post.* Retrieved from http://nationalpost.com/news/canada/what-everybody-got-wrong-about-that-viral-video-of-a-starving-polar-bear

Hubbard, R. (1993). Shock advertising: The Benetton case. *Studies in Popular Culture, 16*(1), 39–51. Retrieved from www.jstor.org/stable/23413769

Iedema, R., Degeling, P., Braithwaite, J., & White, L. (2004). "It's an interesting conversation I'm hearing": The doctor as manager. *Organization Studies, 25*(1), 15–33. doi:10.1177/0170840604038174

Ihlen, Ø. (2002). Rhetoric and resources: Notes for a new approach to public relations and issues management. *Journal of Public Affairs, 2*(4), 259–269. doi:10.1002/pa.118

Innerarity, D. (2010, November 11). La sociedad de los intérpretes. *El País.* Retrieved from www.elpais.com/articulo/ollect/sociedad/interpretes/elpepuopi/20101116 elpepiopi_4/Tes

Innerarity, D. (2011, February 22). Los límites de la transparencia. *El País.* Retrieved from www.elpais.com/articulo/ollect/limites/transparencia/elpepiopi/20110222elpepiopi_4/Tes

Iriart, C., Merhy, E. E., & Waitzkin, H. (2001). Managed care in Latin America: The new common sense in health policy reform. *Social Science & Medicine, 52*, 1243–1253. doi:10.1016/S0277-9536(00)00243-4

ISIS. (2015/1436). The burning of the murtadd pilot. *Dabiq, 7*, 5–8. Retrieved from https://clarionproject.org/docs/islamic-state-dabiq-magazine-issue-7-from-hypocrisy-to-apostasy.pdf

Jaffrelot, C. (1992). Le syncrétisme stratégique et la construction de l'identité nationaliste hindoue. *Revue française de science politique, 42*(4), 594–617. Retrieved from www.persee.fr/doc/rfsp_0035-2950_1992_num_42_4_404327

Jiménez Ure, A. (1998/2015). *Desahuciados.* Mérida, Venezuela: Aleph Universitaria.

Kline, K. N. (2006). A decade of research on health content in the media: The focus on health challenges and sociocultural content and attendant informational and ideological problems. *Journal of Health Communication, 11*(1), 43–59. doi:10.1080/10810730500461067

Katz, E. (2006). Rediscovering Gabriel Tarde. *Political Communication, 23*(3), 263–270. doi:10.1080/10584600600808711

Kayser, W. (1966). *The grotesque in art and literature.* Bloomington, IN & Toronto, ON: Indiana University Press & McGraw-Hill.

Kepel, G. (1991). *La revanche de Dieu: Chrétiens, juifs et musulmans à la recon-quête du monde*. Paris: Éditions du Seuil.

Kepel, G. (2003). Les stratégies islamistes de légitimation de la violence. *Raisons politiques*, *1*(9), 81–95. doi:10.3917/rai.009.0081

Kim, G. (2003–2004). Mikhail Bakhtin: The philosopher of human condition. *Totem*, *12*(1), 53–62. Retrieved from https://ir.lib.uwo.ca/totem/vol12/iss1/8

Kim, S. H., & Willis, L. A. (2007). Talking about obesity: News framing of who is responsible for causing and fixing the problem. *Journal of Health Communica-tion*, *12*(4), 359–376. doi:10.1080/10810730701326051

Koerner, B. I. (2016, April). Why ISIS is winning the social media war. *WIRED*. Retrieved from www.wired.com/2016/03/isis-winning-social-media-war-heres-beat/

Kohlmann, E. F. (2006). The real online terrorist threat. *Foreign Affairs*, *85*(5), 115–124. Retrieved from www.foreignaffairs.com/articles/2006-09-01/real-online-terrorist-threat

Kozak Rovero, G. (2013). Políticas culturales de Estado en la Venezuela del siglo XXI (1999–2013). In M. Bisbal (Ed.), *Saldo en rojo: Comunicaciones y cultura en la era bolivariana* (pp. 293–308). Caracas, Venezuela: Ediciones UCAB—Konrad Adenauer Stiftung.

Kruglanski, A. W., & Orehek, E. (2011). The role of quest for significance in moti-vating terrorism. In J. Forgas, A. Kruglanski, & K. Williams (Eds.), *Social conflict and aggression* (pp. 153–164). New York, NY: Psychology Press.

Lakoff, A. (2005). *Pharmaceutical reason: Knowledge and value in global psychia-try*. Cambridge, UK: Cambridge University Press.

Lash, S. (1995). A reflexividade et seus duplos: estrutura, estética, comunidade. In A. Giddens, U. Beck, & S. Lash (Eds.), *Modernizaçao Reflexiva: Política, Tradiçao e Estética na Ordem Social Moderna* (pp. 135–206). Sao Paulo, Brasil: Editora da UNESP.

Lash, S. (1999). *Another modernity: A different rationality*. Oxford: Blackwell Pub-lishers Inc.

Lash, S. (2002). *Critique of information*. London: Sage Publications.

Latour, B., & Lépinay, V. A. (2009). *The science of passionate interests: An intro-duction to Gabriel Tarde's economic anthropology*. Chicago, IL: Prickly Para-digm Press.

Latour, M. S., Snipes, R. L., & Bliss, S. J. (1996). Don't be afraid to use fear appeals: An experimental study. *Journal of Advertising Research*, *36*(2), 59–67.

Lawrence, T. (1997). AIDS, the problem of representation, and plurality in Derek Jarman's blue. *Social Text*, *52/53*, 241–264. Retrieved from www.jstor.org/stable/466743

Lazzarato, M. (2002). *Puissances de l'invention: La psychologie économique de Gabriel Tarde contre l'économie politique*. Paris: Les Empêcheurs de Penser en Rond.

Le Bon, G. (1905/2001). *Psychologie des foules*. Paris: Félix Alcan, Éditeur (pub-lished in 1905). *Les classiques des sciences sociales* (Université du Québec à Chicoutimi). Retrieved from http://classiques.uqac.ca/classiques/le_bon_gustave/psychologie_des_foules_Alcan/Psycho_des_foules_alcan.pdf

Lecumberri, B. (2012). *La revolución sentimental: Viaje periodístico por la Venezuela de Chávez*. Madrid: Los Libros de la Catarata.

Leibowitz, Y. (1995). *Terre, Peuple, État*. Paris: Plon.

Lemos Martins (de), M. (2011). Médias et mélancolie—le tragique, le baroque et le grotesque. *Sociétés, 111*, 17–25. doi:10.3917/soc.111.0017

Lemos Martins (de), M. (2013). The dead body: Myths, rites and superstitions. *Revista Lusófona de Estudios Culturais/Lusophone Journal of Cultural Studies, 1*(1), 135–160.

Leon, L. (1998). Born again in east LA: The congregation as border space. In R. Stephen Warner & J. Wittner (Eds.), *Gatherings in diaspora: Religious communities and the new immigration* (pp. 163–196). Philadelphia: Temple University Press.

Lévy, B. H. (2003a). *Être juif: Étude lévinassienne*. Paris: Éditions Verdier.

Lévy, B. H. (2003b). *Qui a tué Daniel Pearl?* Paris: Éditions Grasset & Fasquelle.

Lévy, P. (1995). *Qu'est-ce que le virtuel?* Paris: Éditions La Découverte.

Libaert, T. (2003). *La transparence en trompe-l'œil*. Paris: Descartes & Cie.

Linden, I. (2014). Border crossings: Secular versus religious arguments in the public domain. In I. Nahon-Serfaty & R. Ahmed (Eds.), *New media and communication across religions and cultures* (pp. 16–28). Hershey, PA: IGI Global.

Lohr, K. (2012, January 9). Controversy swirls around harsh anti-obesity ads. *NPR*. Retrieved from www.npr.org/2012/01/09/144799538/controversy-swirls-around-harsh-anti-obesity-ads

Lord, K. M. (2006). *The perils and promise of global transparency: Why the information revolution may not lead to security, democracy, or peace*. New York, NY: State University of New York Press.

Lordon, F. (2013). *La société des affects: Pour un structuralisme des passions*. Paris: Éditions du Seuil.

Lupton, D. (2003). *Medicine as culture*. Thousand Oaks, CA: Sage Publications.

Lynch, G. (2012a). *The sacred in the modern world: A cultural sociological approach*. Oxford Scholarship Online. doi:10.1093/acprof:oso/9780199557011.001.0001

Lynch, G. (2012b). Public media and the sacred: A critical perspective. In G. Lynch, J. Mitchell, & A. Strhan (Eds.), *Religion, media and culture: A reader* (pp. 244–250). London, UK & New York, NY: Routledge.

Lynch, M. (2006). Al-Qaeda's media strategies. *National Interest, 83*, 50–56. Retrieved from www.jstor.org/stable/42897599

Machiavel, N. (2009). *Le Prince et autres textes*. Paris: Gallimard & Folio Classique.

MacKenzie, R., Chapman, S., & Holding, S. (2011). Framing responsibility: Coverage of lung cancer among smokers and non-smokers in Australian television news. *Send to Australian and New Zealand Journal of Public Health, 35*(1), 66–70. doi:10.1111/j.1753–6405.2010.00614.x

Macleon, D. (2007, April 7). Benetton Pieta in AIDS campaign. *Inspiration Room*. Retrieved from http://theinspirationroom.com/daily/2007/benetton-pieta-in-aids-campaign/

Martín-Barbero, J. (1993). *Communication, culture and hegemony: From the media to the mediations*. London: Sage Publications.

Martín-Barbero, J. (1997). Mass media as a site of resacralization of contemporary cultures. In S. M. Hoover & K. Lundby (Eds.), *Rethinking media, religion, and culture* (pp. 102–116). Thousand Oaks, CA: Sage Publications. doi:10.4135/9781452243559.n6

Martin-Juchat, F. (2014). La dynamique de marchandisation de la communication affective. *Revue française des sciences de l'information et de la communication*, 5. Retrieved from http://rfsic.revues.org/1012

Martínez, T. E. (1996). *Santa evita*. New York, NY: Vintage Español.

Mayer, J. F. (2008). *Internet et Religion*. Gollion, Switzerland: Infolio.

McBride, P. C. (2005). The value of kitsch. Hermann broch and Robert Musil on art and morality. *Studies in 20th & 21st Century Literature*, *29*(2), 282–301. doi:10.4148/2334-4415.1604

McCall, C., & College, E. (2013). Ambivalent modernities: Foucault's Iranian writings reconsidered. *Foucault Studies*, *15*, 27–51. Retrieved from https://rauli.cbs. dk/index.php/foucault-studies/article/download/3989/4391

McDannell, C. (2012). Scrambling the sacred and the profane. In G. Lynch, J. Mitchell, & A. Strhan (Eds.), *Religion, media and culture: A reader* (pp. 135–146). London, UK & New York, NY: Routledge.

Meijer, A. (2009). Understanding modern transparency. *International Review of Administrative Sciences*, *75*(2), 255–269. doi:10.1177/0020852309104175

Meyer, B. (2012). Religious sensations: Media, aesthetics, and the study of contemporary religion. In G. Lynch, J. Mitchell, & A. Strhan (Eds.), *Religion, media and culture: A reader* (pp. 159–170). London, UK & New York, NY: Routledge.

Milstein, T. (2009). Environmental communication theories. In S. Littlejohn & K. Foss (Eds.), *Encyclopedia of communication theory* (pp. 344–349). Thousand Oaks, CA: Sage Publications.

Moles, A. A. (1971). *Le kitsch: L'art du bonheur*. Paris: Mame.

Molcs, A. A. (1982). El muro de la comunicación. In M. Moragas (de) (Ed.), *Sociología de la comunicación de masas* (pp. 120–135). Barcelona: Editorial Gustavo Gili.

Molleda, J. C. (2010). Authenticity and the construct's dimensions in public relations and communication research. *Journal of Communication Management*, *14*(3), 223–236. doi:10.1108/13632541011064508

Molleda, J. C., & Jain, R. (2013). Testing a perceived authenticity index with triangulation research: The case of Xcaret in Mexico. *International Journal of Strategic Communication*, *7*(1), 1–20. doi:10.1080/1553118X.2012.725233

Morales, M. (2013). The People Show: La historia televisada de un presidente. In M. Bisbal (Ed.), *Saldo en rojo. Comunicaciones y cultura en la era bolivariana* (pp. 209–225). Caracas, Venezuela: Ediciones UCAB—Konrad Adenauer Stiftung.

Morley, J. (2006, July 27). What is Hezbollah? *washingtonpost.com*. Retrieved from www.washingtonpost.com/wpdyn/content/article/2006/07/17/AR2006071700912. html

Mowlana, H. (1979). Technology versus tradition: Communication in the Iranian revolution. *Journal of Communication*, *29*(3), 107–112. doi:10.1111/j.1460-2466. 1979.tb01718.x

Nahon-Serfaty, I. (1999). Del Sida como metáfora al Sida como "commodity". *Comunicación*, *106*, 60–63.

Nahón Serfaty, I. (2010). Actualidad del mito de la Independencia: en búsqueda de sentido en la Babel fragmentada. In I. Nahón Serfaty, P. Correa, S. Pinardi, J. C.

Reyes, G. J. Villasmil, E. Aliendres, C. Andara, & G. Bottoni (Eds.), *Detrás del mito: La Independencia de Venezuela 200 años después* (pp. 21–45). Caracas, Venezuela: Banesco.

Nahon-Serfaty, I. (2012). The disruptive consequences of discourse fragmentation in the organization and delivery of health care: A look into diabetes. *Health Communication, 27*(5), 506–516. doi:10.1080/10410236.2011.618426

Nayan, S. (2013). Interrupting images: A rhetorical analysis of Greenpeace's advertising tactics. *GSTF International Journal on Media & Communications (JMC), 1*(1), 113–119.

NPR. (2016, October 9). Fact check: Clinton and Trump debate for the 2nd time. *NPR.* Retrieved from www.npr.org/2016/10/09/497056227/fact-check-clinton-and-trump-debate-for-the-second-time

Oliva, C. (1978). *Antecedentes estéticos del esperpento.* Murcia, España: Ediciones, 23–27.

Oliver, R. W. (2004). *What is transparency?* New York, NY: McGraw-Hill.

Oliviero, Toscani. (2008). https://news.syr.edu/2008/03/photographer-oliviero-toscani-to-address-issues-of-ethics-and-social-responsibility-in-art-at-su-florence/

Open Society Justice Initiative. (2016). *Eroding trust: The UK's prevent counter-extremism strategy in health and education.* New York, NY: Open Society Foundations.

Ortega y Gasset, J. (1929/2012). *La rebelión de las masas.* Barcelona: Espasa Lobros.

Palmer, S. (2014). Cult wars on the internet: Virtual battles and the challenges of cyberspace. In I. Nahon-Serfaty & R. Ahmed (Eds.), *New media and communication across religions and cultures* (pp. 99–108). Hershey, PA: IGI Global.

Parry, V. (2003). The art of branding a condition. *Medical Marketing & Media, 38,* 43–49.

Pasquali, A. (2005). *18 ensayos sobre comunicaciones.* Caracas, Venezuela: Debate.

Payne, L. (1992). *Disease-mongers: How doctors, drug companies and insurers are making you feel sick.* New York, NY: Wiley & Sons.

Peraza, A. (2013). El discurso del Mesías davídico en Chávez. In M. Bisbal (Ed.), *La Política y sus tramas. Miradas desde la Venezuela del presente* (pp. 163–166). Caracas, Venezuela: Ediciones de la UCAB.

Peterson, A. (2016, July 12). Holocaust Museum to visitors: Please stop catching Pokémon here. *The Washington Post.* Retrieved from www.washingtonpost.com/news/the-switch/wp/2016/07/12/holocaust-museum-to-visitors-please-stop-catching-pokemon-here/?utm_term=.90c241328dae

Pezé, E. (2002). L'émir, l'image, l'Islam. *Les cahiers de médiologie, 13,* 173–180. Retrieved from www.cairn.info/revue-les-cahiers-de-mediologie-2002-1-page-173.htm

Pino Iturrieta, E. (2003). *El divino Bolívar: Ensayo sobre una religión republicana.* Madrid: Catarata.

Pino Iturrieta, E. (2013). La revolución bolivariana: principio ó fin de una época? In M. Bisbal (Ed.), *Saldo en rojo: Comunicaciones y cultura en la era bolivariana* (pp. 13–18). Caracas, Venezuela: Ediciones UCAB—Konrad Adenauer Stiftung.

Powell, D., & Leiss, W. (1997). *Mad cows and mother's milk: The perils of poor risk communication.* Montreal: McGill-Queen's University Press.

Prosser, H. (2010). Marvelous medicines and dangerous drugs: The representation of prescription medicine in the UK newsprint media. *Public Understanding of Science, 19*(1), 52–69. doi:10.1177/0963662508094100

Puhl, R., Peterson, J. L., & Luedicke, J. (2013). Fighting obesity or obese persons? Public perceptions of obesity-related health messages. *International Journal of Obesity, 37*(6), 774–782. doi:10.1038/ijo.2012.156

Rancière, J. (2007). *The future of the image.* London, UK & New York, NY: Verso.

Rancière, J. (2009). *The emancipated spectator.* London: Verson & New Left Books.

Rangel, C. (1976/2005). *Del buen salvaje al buen revolucionario: Mitos y realidades de América Latina.* Caracas, Venezuela: Criteria Editorial.

Reyna, F. (2013). La Sociedad Civil en el Contexto Post Electoral. In M. Bisbal (Ed.), *La Política y sus tramas:* Miradas desde la Venezuela del presente (pp. 180–189). Caracas, Venezuela: Ediciones de la UCAB.

Rogers, E. M. (1998). When the mass media have strong effects: Intermedia processes. In J. Trent (Ed.), *Communication: Views from the helm for the twenty-first century* (pp. 276–285). Boston, MA: Allyn and Bacon.

Rosa Gualda, R. J. (2012). *The discourse of Hugo Chávez in "Aló Presidente": Establishing the bolivarian revolution through television performance.* PhD dissertation, University of Texas at Austin.

Roy, O. (2008). *La sainte ignorance: Le temps de la réligion sans culture.* Paris: Éditions du Seuil.

Safar, E. (2013). El Aló Presidente y las cadenas de radio y television Espejos de la pasión autoritaria del presidente Chávez. In M. Bisbal (Ed.), *Saldo en rojo: Comunicaciones y cultura en la era bolivariana* (pp. 226–249). Caracas, Venezuela: Ediciones UCAB—Konrad Adenauer Stiftung.

Safranski, R. (1999). *Le Mal ou le Théâtre de la liberté.* Paris: Bernard Grasset.

Scalvini, M. (2010). Glamorizing sick bodies: How commercial advertising has changed the representation of HIV/AIDS. *Social Semiotics, 20*(3), 219–231. doi:10.1080/10350331003722570

Schevill, J. (1977/2009). The American and European grotesque: Notes on the grotesque: Anderson, Brecht and Williams. In H. Bloom & B. Hobby (Eds.), The grotesque (pp. 1–12). New York, NY: Bloom's Literary Criticism.

Schill, D. (2012). The visual image and the political image: A review of visual communication research in the field of political communication. *The Review of Communication, 12*(2), 118–142. doi:10.1080/15358593.2011.653504

Silva-Ferrer, M. (2013). Migraciones culturales en los 14 años de Hugo Chávez. In M. Bisbal (Ed.), *Saldo en rojo: Comunicaciones y cultura en la era bolivariana* (pp. 274–292). Caracas, Venezuela: Ediciones UCAB—Konrad Adenauer Stiftung.

Sismondo, S. (2004). Pharmaceutical maneuvers. *Social Studies of Science, 34*(2), 149–159. doi:10.1177/0306312704042575

Sontag, S. (1977). *Illness as metaphor.* New York, NY: Farrar, Strauss and Giroux.

Sontag, S. (2004, May 23). Regarding the torture of others. *The New York Times Magazine.* Retrieved from www.nytimes.com/2004/05/23/magazine/regarding-the-torture-of-others.html)

Spinoza (de), B. (1677/2014). *A political treatise*. Adelaide, SA: University of Adelaide. Retrieved from https://ebooks.adelaide.edu.au/s/spinoza/benedict/political/complete.html)

Stern, J., & Berger, J. M. (2015). *ISIS: The state of terror*. New York, NY: Ecco & HarperCollins Publishers.

Stevens, M. (2017, December 11). Video of starving polar bear "rips your heart out of your chest". *The New York Times*. Retrieved from www.nytimes.com/2017/12/11/world/canada/starving-polar-bear.html?smid=tw-nytimes&smtyp=cur

Strathern, M. (2000). The tyranny of transparency. *British Educational Research Journal, 26*(3), 309–321. doi:10.1080/713651562

Strati, A. (1996). Organizations viewed through the lens of aesthetics. Organization. *EssaysonAestheticandOrganization,3*(2),209–218.doi:10.1177/135050849632004

Sturken, M., & Cartwright, L. (2009). *Practices of looking: An introduction to visual culture*. New York, NY & Oxford: Oxford University Press.

Tait, S. (2008). Pornographies of violence? Internet spectatorship on body horror. *Critical Studies in Media Communication, 25*(1), 91–111. doi:10.1080/15295030701851148

Tarde, G. (1902/2006). *Psychologie économique: Tome premier*. Paris: Félix Alcan, Éditeur (published in 1902). *Les classiques des sciences sociales* (Université du Québec à Chicoutimi). Retrieved from http://classiques.uqac.ca/classiques/tarde_gabriel/psycho_economique_t1/psycho_economique_t1.pdf

Tawil-Souri, H. (2012). "War on terror" in the Arab Media. In D. Freedman & D. Thussu (Eds.), *Media and terrorism: Global perspectives* (pp. 241–254). London: Sage Publications.

Tchakhotine, S. (1992). *Le viol des foules par la propaganda politique*. Paris: Gallimard.

Tenner, E. (1997). *Why things bite back? Technology and the revenge of unintended consequences*. New York, NY: Vintage Books.

Tessier, R., & Prades, J. A. (1991). *Le Sacré*. Paris, France & Anjou, Québec: Éditions du Cerf—Éditions Fides.

Tewksbury, D. (2005). The seeds of audience fragmentation: Specialization in the use of online news sites. *Journal of Broadcasting & Electronic Media, 49*(3), 332–348. doi:10.1207/s15506878jobem4903_5

Torres, A. T. (2009). *La herencia de la tribu: Del mito de la Independencia a la Revolución Bolivariana*. Caracas, Venezuela: Editorial Alfa.

Tsoukas, H. (1997). The tyranny of light: The temptations and the paradoxes of the information society. *Futures, 29*(9), 827–843. doi:10.1016/S0016-3287(97)00035-9

Valle-Inclán, R. M. (1981). *Luces de bohemia: Esperpento*. Madrid: Espasa-Calpe S.A.

Vasconcellos-Silva, P. R., Uribe Rivera, F. J., & Siebeneichler, F. B. (2007). Healthcare organizations, linguistic communities, and the emblematic model of palliative care. *Cad. Saúde Pública, 23*(7), 1529–1538. doi:10.1590/S0102-311X2007000700003

Venezuelan Ministry of Information and Communication. (2010). Exhuma Venzuela restora. *teleSUR tv*. Retrieved from https://www.youtube.com/watch?v=1oGI0sSTsHY

Warraq, I. (2009, February). Apologists of totalitarianism: From communism to Islam, part III. Michel Foucault. *New English Review*. Retrieved from www.newenglishreview.org/Ibn_Warraq/Apologists_of_Totalitarianism%3A_From_Communism_to_Islam,_Part_III/

Weber, M. (1978). *Economy and society: An outline of interpretative sociology* (G. Roth & C. Wittich, Eds.). Berkeley & Los Angeles, CA: University of California Press.

Wente, M. (2017, December 11). The starving polar bear raises a question: Is fake news okay for a good cause? *Globe & Mail*. Retrieved from www.theglobeandmail.com/opinion/is-fake-news-okay-if-the-cause-is-good/article37290997/

Wiley, L. F. (2013). Shame, blame, and the emerging law of obesity control. *University of California, Davis Law Review*, *47*(1), 121–188. Retrieved from https://lawreview.law.ucdavis.edu/issues/47/1/Articles/47-1_Wiley.pdf

Zaretsky, R. (2017a, February 20). Trump and the "society of the spectacle ". *The New York Times*. Retrieved from www.nytimes.com/2017/02/20/opinion/trump-and-the-society-of-the-spectacle.html

Zaretsky, R. D. (2017b, July 3). Return of the grotesque. *Aeon*. Retrieved from https://aeon.co/essays/the-grotesque-is-back-but-this-time-no-one-is-laughing

Ziv, S. (2015, January 29). France launches online offensive to prevent jihadist recruitment. *Newsweek*. Retrieved from www.newsweek.com/france-launches-online-offensive-prevent-jihadist-recruitment-303079

Index

About the Author

Isaac Nahon-Serfaty is Associate Professor in the Department of Communication at the University of Ottawa, Canada. This book is part of a research programme about the economy of emotions in public communication.

For Product Safety Concerns and Information please contact our EU
representative GPSR@taylorandfrancis.com Taylor & Francis Verlag GmbH,
Kaufingerstraße 24, 80331 München, Germany

Printed and bound by CPI Group (UK) Ltd, Croydon, CR0 4YY
11/04/2025
01844008-0004